Religious and Poetic Experience
in the Thought of
Michael Oakeshott

imprint-academic.com/idealists

Religious and Poetic Experience in the Thought of Michael Oakeshott

Glenn Worthington

ia

imprint-academic.com

Published in the UK by Imprint Academic
PO Box 200, Exeter EX5 5YX, UK

Published in the USA by Imprint Academic
Philosophy Documentation Center
PO Box 7147, Charlottesville, VA 22906-7147, USA

ISBN 0 907845 62 2

A CIP catalogue record for this book is available from the
British Library and US Library of Congress

imprint-academic.com/idealists

Contents

Acknowledgements

I would like to express my indebtedness to David West, who supervised my thesis and gave much of his attention to the detail as well as the overall argument that is presented here.[1] The work owes much, not only to the time spent in conversation with Luke O'Sullivan, a fellow doctoral scholar of Oakeshott's thought at the Australian National University, but also to his generous sharing of research materials which he had gathered for his own doctoral studies. Jim George and Jeremy Shearmur of the Department of Political Science also gave their time in reading the work.

David Boucher extended his help and generous hospitality whilst I was on fieldwork in Britain in 1994. And the comments of Peter Nicholson, Richard Flathman and Conal Condren who examined the thesis provided many helpful suggestions on how the text could be improved as well as encouragement to continue exploring lines of inquiry that opened during my studies. I would also like to express my gratitude to Christel

---

[1]   *The Civil Philosophy of Michael Oakeshott: A Theology of Identity*, (Canberra, Australian National University, 1997).

Oakeshott for allowing me to look over her husband's personal library.

Finally, I am grateful for the time allowed me by the Department of the House of Representatives of the Commonwealth Parliament of Australia and the facilities extended to me by the School of Social Sciences at the Australian National University to bring the thesis to publication standard.

Chapter 1
Introduction

1. Why Study Oakeshott's Account of Religious and Poetic Experience?

The following work is an attempt to set out, in its most comprehensive terms, Oakeshott's characterisation of conduct in terms of the good life; that is his account of what it is to live well. I have described this as a study of Oakeshott's account of the good life to indicate the scope of the subject matter covered. It signals an intention to deal with more than Oakeshott's characterisation of the terms of moral association or political activity, it sets as a frame of reference his understanding and diagnosis of the human condition and modern responses to this predicament.

A passage from one of C. S. Lewis's broadcast talks provides a more detailed map of the scope and structure of the following study. Lewis identified morality as being properly concerned with three things:

> Firstly, with fair play and harmony between individuals. Secondly, with what might be called tidying up or harmonising the things inside each individual. Thirdly with the general purpose of life as a whole: what man was made for.

He went on to observe that 'modern people are nearly always thinking about the first thing [but they] forget the other two.'[1] I shall explore Oakeshott's understanding of the good life in terms of all three areas of morality identified by Lewis: his characterisation of moral association between individuals; the character of the personae that engage in this type of association; and the sense in which he thought it appropriate to talk of a purpose that is general to life as a whole.

It is my contention then, that Oakeshott's work does not suffer the modern obsession identified by Lewis of confining moral considerations to the appropriate terms of association. However, much of the secondary literature on Oakeshott could be taken as proving the point to which I am claiming his work is an exception. Most of the scholarly attention that has been devoted to Oakeshott's account of conduct has focused upon his characterisation of the relations that constitute moral association between individuals and the type of political activity appropriate to these relations. Comparatively little effort has been made to address his account of the type of person (or character) that is capable of entering into and enjoying moral association or whether anything like a purpose that is general to life can be found in his work. When these two other areas of Oakeshott's account of conduct have been noticed, they have tended to be used either to re-iterate or expand upon points being made about his characterisation of the appropriate terms of association. The following exercise, then, consists in an effort to identify Oakeshott's characterisation of conduct in terms of each of the three aspects of morality outlined by Lewis and it does so by attending to his writings on religious and poetic experience together with the better known of his tracts on moral association and political activity.

A proposal to consider Oakeshott's account of the good life using his writings on religious and poetic experience may

---

[1]   C.S. Lewis, *Mere Christianity*, (Glasgow, Fontana Books, 1975), pp. 66–7.

strike readers who are familiar with his work as a somewhat eccentric or even misguided approach. It might be pointed out that he wrote relatively little on either subject. A more productive approach, on this line of understanding, would concentrate upon the subjects on which Oakeshott himself focused. Undeniably, he wrote more extensively on the character of moral association and political activity than religious or poetic experience (hence the common recognition of him as first and foremost a moral or, even more frequently, a political theorist). The implication is that his accounts of morality and politics reveal more of his characterisation of the good life than his reflections upon religious and poetic experience.

The above argument suffers two shortcomings. First and most seriously, it misconstrues the character of Oakeshott's approach to thinking. Oakeshott did not characterise identities, such as 'conduct' or 'the good life', as collections of individual parts that when brought together form a whole. The various subjects on which he reflected are not individual, self-contained components that can be understood in isolation from one another; they do not form a cumulative whole in the way that individual stones, when stacked together, form a pile.[2] Rather, political, moral, religious and poetic experience are identities that provide a series of lenses or frames of reference that comprehend, in lesser and greater degrees, the good life as a whole. Thus, politics is not a separate sphere of activity within the good life, rather it is a particular manner of reflecting upon and enacting the good life and this is so of moral, religious and poetic experience. Each frame of reference understands the good life variously as a political, a moral, a religious and a poetic whole. Proposing to explore Oakeshott's characterisation of the good life through his writings on reli-

---

[2] See R.L. Nettleship, *Philosophical Remains*, 2nd edition (ed. A.C. Bradley) (London, Macmillan, 1901), pp. 33-8. I found a copy of Nettleship's *Philosophical Remains* in Oakeshott's personal library when visiting the cottage at Acton in 1994.

gious and poetic experience challenges the (at least implicit) view amongst many commentators on his work that his writings on moral association and politics provide the most adequate available terms in which to understand his characterisation of conduct.

Arguing that Oakeshott's writings on moral association and political activity are more significant than those on religious and poetic experience, simply on the grounds that he wrote a greater volume on morality and politics, offers no reflection of the weight that he attributed to each of these frames of reference. The weight of significance rather than the volume of writing refers to what he actually understood by each frame of reference and its relation to the others. Each frame of reference provides a more or less comprehensive view of the good life so that the more comprehensive frames include (that is, they comprehend) the less comprehensive. And on Oakeshott's view, the character of politics constitutes a less comprehensive view of the good life than the terms of moral association, and the terms of moral association constitute a less comprehensive view of good life than religious or poetic experience.

So the following exercise sets out to interpret Oakeshott's work by placing the common understanding of it as primarily concerned with the appropriate terms of moral association and political activity in a more comprehensive religious and poetic context. This does not entail rejecting current understandings of Oakeshott's writings on moral association and politics, but rather it seeks to place these endeavours in a more comprehensive context. I am not arguing that Oakeshott's political and moral philosophy is of no significance in understanding his characterisation of the good life but that his idea of the good life has a more complete religious and poetic significance. A second response to objections that Oakeshott wrote relatively little on religious and poetic experience observes that he actually wrote more on these subjects than is often recognised. The extent of his writings on religious and poetic experience will become apparent when they are considered in detail in the body of this work.

2. The Argument

The following study is divided into four chapters. They consider, in turn, Oakeshott's characterisations of the first principles of experience, or metaphysics; religious experience; moral association; and poetic experience. Beginning with a consideration of Oakeshott's metaphysics provides a context in which to understand his characterisation of specific types or orders of experience. Oakeshott argued that truth and reality, at least in their most comprehensive and complete forms, are distinct from truth and reality as they are presupposed in orders of what he called abstract experience. The type of experience that arises in living one's life, which Oakeshott specified as the world conceived *sub specie voluntatis* – the world conceived under the species of will – is one such order of abstract experience (2.1). The presuppositions that underlie the world conceived *sub specie voluntatis* imply the character of truth and reality is change and that identity is constituted in terms of separateness from other identities (2.2). The understandings in terms of which we conduct ourselves is the stuff of the world conceived *sub specie voluntatis*. Among the postulates Oakeshott identified as underlying conduct are the substantive and formal aspects of an action. These postulates provide a basis for exploring his account of the character of two modern responses to the human predicament (2.3).

The consideration of Oakeshott's accounts of religious experience, moral association and poetic experience provide frames of reference that correspond respectively to the second, first and third categories of moral consideration identified by Lewis. Oakeshott's characterisation of religious experience conveys his most comprehensive account of the terms in which moderns have valued the self – religious experience refers to nothing less than the salvation or damnation of a self. Oakeshott understood modern responses to the human predicament in terms of two moral characters – the individual and the anti-individual (3.1). He also identified two possible conceptions of salvation available to a self: the condition of being saved either within the present or in a future condition (3.2). Each of these conceptions of salvation reflects a distinct idea of the self that Oakeshott elucidated in terms of postulates that the individual and the anti-individual make about the character of a moral self (3.3). Oakeshott's account of the postulates underlying the ideas of self held by the individual and the anti-individual suggest that the individual understands salvation in terms of a present condition and the anti-individual understands salvation in terms of a future condition (3.4).

Oakeshott's characterisation of moral association presents moral relations between individuals as appropriately understood in terms of their authority, rather than their desirability. The propriety of understanding moral association in terms of its authority is reflected in considering the appropriate principle in terms of which the modern state is constituted. Confusing the authority of the terms of moral association with their desirability indicates a morality approving of the anti-individual (4.1). Understanding moral association as constituted primarily in terms of authority does not exclude consideration of these conditions in terms of their desirability, an activity Oakeshott defined as politics. Attending to considerations of the authoritative conditions of moral association in terms of their desirability bears out the vital, that is present, character of these conditions (4.2). Oakeshott identified the complex character of modern politics in terms of two political styles; the politics of faith and the politics of scepticism. A politics of faith unqualified by a politics of scepticism is liable to reduce the terms in which a state is constituted to their desirability. The self-defeat inherent in an unqualified politics of faith reveals in its most graphic form the unsustainability of moral association understood in terms of desirability (4.3).

Finally, what might be phrased a purpose that is general to life can be discerned in one of the aspects in which Oakeshott cast his account(s) of poetic experience. Before exploring Oakeshott's characterisation of a purpose that is general to life, however, a number of not necessarily consistent views of poetic experience need to be distinguished in his writings. In one mood Oakeshott identified poetic experience with religious experience in understanding both to arise in a self that understands moral achievement in terms of the integrity of the sensibility or motive in which it acts, rather than the gaining of external goals (5.1). In another mood Oakeshott's writings trace the development of a philosophical argument for the autonomy of poetic images from other orders of experience, particularly the order of experience in terms of which we conduct ourselves (5.2). A third understanding of poetic experience can also be detected in Oakeshott's writings. Poetic experience is understood as arising in the reflection upon the self-understandings that a society has of itself. These reflections refer to a predicament that may be recognised as general to life. While the substance of particular poetic reflections invariably occurs within the contingencies of a local situation, in being recognised as referring to a predicament that is general to life they intimate a purpose that is general to life (5.3).

I am not claiming that Oakeshott's responses to the three categories of moral consideration identified by Lewis equate in any significant way with what Lewis may have thought adequate. Lewis's categories are deployed as structural props rather than substantive measures of satisfactoriness. And it should be recognised at the outset that there is a fundamental difference in the writings of the two thinkers. Lewis was engaged in apologetics – he was concerned to justify a particular position and set of responses to the human predicament over others. Oakeshott was engaged in understanding what responses have been made without justifying this or that particular body of beliefs. However, in exploring Oakeshott's account of the appropriate terms in which selves and associations between selves are constituted as well as the sense in which it makes to refer to a purpose that is general to life, his writings contribute to a tradition of thought in which Lewis can be located; the tradition that Oakeshott called the morality of the individual.

Chapter 2

The Absolute, Life and Conduct

In an unpublished typescript dated 1925 Oakeshott declared the importance of setting in order the first principles of experience before proceeding to treat of the character of this or that particular experience or type of experience: 'the most important problems of political philosophy are solved or mis-solved while the mind is still occupied with metaphysics before it ever reaches politics properly so called'.[1] This statement is consistent with the attention he gave to metaphysics early in his publishing career. The only book-length treatise that he ever published is a consideration of the character of experience without presupposition, reservation, arrest or modification, what he called philosophical experience.[2] While *Experience and Its Modes* constitutes Oakeshott's most comprehensive statement of the first principles of experience, he returned to con-

[1]   M. Oakeshott, *A Discussion of Some Matters Preliminary to a Study of Political Philosophy*, (Unpublished, 1925), p. 3.

[2]   M. Oakeshott, *Experience and Its Modes*, (Cambridge, Cambridge University Press, 1985) p. 2.

sider and restate his thoughts on this subject many times throughout his career. Evidence of his on-going effort to clarify and specify the first principles of experience can be found in 'The Conception of a Philosophical Jurisprudence', 'The Concept of a Philosophy of Politics', 'Political Philosophy', *The Voice of Poetry in the Conversation of Mankind* and 'On the Theoretical Understanding of Human Conduct'.[3]

A thorough consideration of Oakeshott's characterisation of the first principles of experience would require a study devoted solely to this subject. It would need to canvass his account of the characteristics of philosophical, historical, scientific, practical and poetic experience and the relation of each of these types of experience to the others. It would also need to take account of the vigorous debate among commentators on Oakeshott's work concerning the character of the relations between each of these orders of experience and particularly the relation and status of philosophical experience to other abstract modes of experience, as well as the consistency with which he held these views throughout his long publishing career.[4] Not least of the issues that have provoked debate among commentators is his view of the relations of theoretical reflection upon the character of conduct to conduct, his contribution to the so-called theory-praxis debate.[5]

---

[3]   'The Concept of a Philosophical; Jurisprudence', *Politca*, 3 (1938), pp. 203–22 and 345–60; 'The Concept of a Political Philosophy' and 'Political Philosophy'. in *Religion, Politics and the Moral Life* (ed. T. Fuller) (New Haven, Yale University Press, 1993) pp. 119–37 and 138–55; *The Voice of Poetry in the Conversation of Mankind*, (London, Bowes and Bowes, 1959), pp. 63; 'On the Theoretical Understanding of Human Conduct' in *On Human Conduct*, (Oxford, Clarendon Press, 1975), pp. 1– 107.

[4]   For instance, T. Modood, 'Oakeshott's Conception of Philosophy', *History of Political Thought*, 1 (1980), pp. 315–22 and D. Boucher, 'Overlap and Autonomy: The Different Worlds of Collingwood and Oakeshott', *Storia*, 4 (1989).

[5]   For instance, D. Hall and T. Modood, 'Oakeshott and the Impossibility of a Philosophical Politics', *Political Studies*, 30 (1982), pp. 157–76 and

The above issues must be of concern to any scholar of Oakeshott's thought. However as I have said, to enter into a full consideration of them would require a complete study in itself. This said, however, an account of some of the elements of Oakeshott's account of metaphysics is not entirely out of place here. At the very least an account of what Oakeshott understood as constituting the defining criterion of experience will set a context for considering his account of the type of experience that arises from, and is constituted by, the understandings in terms of which we conduct our lives. Accordingly, the following chapter begins with an account of Oakeshott's characterisation of truth and reality in their most comprehensive terms and as distinguished from truth and reality as manifest in other orders of experience. Following the parlance of the British Idealists, whose approach to thinking and style of exposition held heavy sway over the pre-World War Two Oakeshott, the first section of the chapter considers the distinction between concrete and abstract experience. It is important to grasp precisely what Oakeshott meant by describing experience in terms of absolute and abstract formations particularly as a preliminary to considering his characterisation of religious experience with its connotations of eternity and infinity and their relation to the temporal and finite. The second section considers Oakeshott's account of the specific order of experience that arises when the world is conceived as a species of will. Both the first and second sections of the chapter refer heavily to *Experience and Its Modes*. I hold, without explicitly making the case here, that Oakeshott adhered consistently to his account of the first principles of experience enunciated in *Experience and Its Modes* throughout

---

J. Liddington, 'Hall and Modood on Oakeshott', *Political Studies*, 30 (1982), pp. 177–83.

the remainder of his long publishing career.[6] The final section of the chapter considers Oakeshott's account of two postulates underlying conduct as providing reference points for selves seeking to constitute themselves as identities in conduct.

1. The Absolute and Abstraction

Oakeshott introduced *Experience and Its Modes* as 'not so much an apology for Idealism as a restatement of its first principles.'[7] A core characteristic of the Idealist position to which Oakeshott referred was an argument that the understandings in terms of which we live our lives are abstractions of and thus distinct from concrete reality, which remains hidden at this level of experience. We might profitably begin by inquiring after what Oakeshott meant by describing experience in terms of its 'abstractness' and 'concreteness'.

Oakeshott's restatement of the first principles of Idealism is underpinned by a coherence theory of truth.[8] Coherence theories are thus designated in order to distinguish them from correspondence theories of truth. Needless to say, both accounts of truth are far more sophisticated than the brief outlines I present here. To follow the complexities and subtleties of each theory, however, would take us far from the task at hand. For present purposes they are important for the basis they provide for two different conceptions of reality. In both theories, truth is the criterion that distinguishes what is real from what is not real.

---

[6]   I have argued the case for the consistency of Oakeshott's metaphysics at length in the first two chapters of my doctoral dissertation, Worthington, *The Civil Philosophy of Michael Oakeshott*.

[7]   *Experience and Its Modes*, p. 7.

[8]   For Oakeshott's rendition of the coherence theory of truth see *Ibid.*, pp. 33-7. A fuller account of the coherence theory of truth is provided in H.H. Joachim, *The Nature of Truth*, 2nd edition (ed. R.G. Collingwood) (London, Oxford University Press, 1939).

Correspondence theories of truth posit a world that is external to and independent of a subject's consciousness of that world. Truth arises when a subject makes judgements about the world that correspond to the world's real character. Correspondence theories of truth suppose that we are born *tabula rasa*; we have no innate ideas. Reality is external to the experiencing subject and we come to know reality through sense perceptions out of which we form ideas about the world which caused them. A subject can be understood on the analogy of a mechanism which perceives reality either correctly or mistakenly. Truth describes the judgements of a subject that correspond to external reality.

Coherence theories of truth deny the ascertainability and so the relevance to truth of any world that is external or independent of an experiencing subject. On coherence accounts, truth is what is coherent with or implied in that which is already within a subject's experience. A subject's world is coeval with the coming into being of that subject. Thus, Oakeshott argued that 'a theory of knowledge which is not at the same time a theory of being is an impossibility.[9] We do not begin from the raw data of sense perceptions, as builders begin with bricks and mortar, and then arrange these perceptions into a world corresponding to the external situation:

> Thinking, according to the analogy of *Theaetetus*, is a process of catching not wild birds, not what is outside experience (such as the objects in mere sensation), but tame birds already within the cage of the mind.[10]

----

[9]   *Experience and Its Modes*, pp. 348–9.

[10]   *Ibid.*, p. 19. Oakeshott acknowledged that tame birds still suppose the prior existence of birds once wild. This is a problem with the analogy, not the argument. Cf. F.H. Bradley, *The Principles of Logic*, 2nd edition (London, Oxford University Press, 1922), Vol. 1, Bk. 1, Sect. 2, p. 2, 'not only are we unable to judge before we use ideas, but, strictly speaking we cannot judge till we use them as ideas.' For Bradley, as Oakeshott, judgement is synonymous with experience.

Our world is concomitant with our understanding of it.

Far from being born blank into an unknown world, we are born of a world of experience – each of us is his or her experience of reality. Rather than beings possessing potential capacities for certain types of experience, we are understood in our capacity as beings, to be experiencing beings. The world (and so the self) is not so much a blank slate as a semi-legible scrawl which we attempt to understand and write more legibly.[11] Our attempts at understanding ourselves and our world consist in organising our partially understood experience more coherently by discovering 'facts' which lie implicit in our experience. Coherence theories of truth posit a world of given experience out of which a world of greater coherence and completeness may be achieved. As experience becomes more explicitly coherent it becomes more complete, which is to say more real.[12] The absolute dichotomy between truth and falsity, reality and unreality is rejected for a conception of degrees of truth and reality.[13]

Coherence theories of truth presented in works such as Hegel's *Phenomenology of Spirit*, Bradley's *Appearance and Reality* and Oakeshott's *Experience and Its Modes* do not propose a dichotomy between, on the one hand, 'Spirit', 'Reality' and 'Experience' as principles of truth and, on the other, 'phenomena', 'appearances' and 'modes' as principles of non-truth. Spirit is phenomenal and every phenomenon is a partial manifestation of Spirit; Reality is its appearances and every appear-

---

[11] See *On Human Conduct*, pp. 1–8 for Oakeshott's account of the way in which the world becomes more intelligible.

[12] See *Experience and Its Modes*, pp. 33–4, 'What is achieved in experience … is a world of ideas which … is unified, and because it is unified, is complete.'

[13] Characteristically, Oakeshott did not dismiss correspondence theories of truth out of hand but finds that correspondence is ultimately coherent. *Ibid.*, p. 40, 'The only absolute in experience is a complete and unified world of ideas, and for experience to correspond with that is but to correspond with itself; and that is what I mean by coherence.'

ance is an appearance of Reality; and Experience is modal and every mode is a mode of Experience. Spirit, Reality and Experience do not exclude phenomena, appearances and modes. Rather, Spirit, Reality and Experience represent the concrete whole of experience of which phenomena, appearances and modes are abstractions. And in so far as an abstraction provides a partial view of the concrete whole of experience, it is a partial view of reality and thus partially real.

Concrete experience arises out of our given experience 'when it is absolved or emancipated from the necessity of finding its significance in relations with what is outside itself.'[14] A world of concrete experience is achieved in the unrelenting determination to discover unquestioned presuppositions that underlie what is given in experience. The procedure of inquiring after the presuppositions underlying a given world of experience (and thus the character of that world) ceases only when a world of experience no longer merely posits presuppositions about the character of reality, that is, when the character of reality has been made completely explicit. The critical procedure of interrogating the presuppositions, on which a world of experience rests enlarges, completes and unifies experience in more coherent worlds of achieved experience. In achieving progressively more complete and unified worlds of experience, the defining criterion underlying all experience becomes, by degrees, more explicit. Oakeshott referred to this defining criterion of all experience variously as 'the concrete whole of experience' and 'the world of absolute ideas'.[15] The adjectives 'concrete' and 'absolute' indicate a quality of experience that rejects all presupposition, circumstance and contingency. Absolute truth is implied by every experiencing subject and in every world of experience.

---

[14] *Ibid.*, p. 47.

[15] *Ibid.*, pp. 46–7 and p. 348.

Concrete experience is pursued in what Oakeshott called a philosophical manner of understanding. He indicated the 'absolute' quality of philosophical experience by describing philosophy as giving rise to the world conceived *sub specie aeternitatis* – the world conceived under the species of eternity. In referring to a world conceived *sub specie aeternitatis* he indicated that philosophy must always prefer what is necessary in experience to what is contingent, what is concrete to what is abstract and what is more coherent to what is less coherent. He described the world of absolute experience that arises from the philosophical interrogation of the presuppositions underlying what is given in experience as 'experience without presupposition, reservation, arrest or modification.'[16] A world of philosophical experience is:

> experience which is self-conscious and self-critical throughout, in which the determination to remain unsatisfied with anything short of a completely coherent world of ideas is absolute and unqualified ... It is merely experience become critical of itself, experience sought and followed for its own sake.'[17]

Philosophical experience, then, arises in a refusal to cease interrogating the presuppositions that are implied in a world of experience until every implication has been revealed in all its explicitness.

At no point in philosophy are presuppositions about the character of reality left unexamined. To do so would allow the possibility of a world of (partial) experience (an appearance of reality) to crystalize upon the presuppositions. A world built upon unquestioned presuppositions would express less than the absolute character of reality. Reality (and truth), then, achieves its fullest character in the philosophical activity of self-critically explicating the assumptions that are implicit in a world of given experience. To achieve this 'absolute' charac-

---

[16]   *Ibid.*, p. 2.
[17]   *Ibid.*, p. 82.

ter, philosophical activity must be self-critical throughout and thus, the activity of philosophising has no conclusion.

Oakeshott's characterisation of philosophical experience as a world of absolute ideas or concrete reality or, indeed, as the world conceived *sub specie aeternitatis* conveys more than a vague sense of the religious. However, any suggestion that he thought of philosophical endeavour as an engagement to establish the existence of God or to discover His attributes, such as is traditionally considered to be the proper purview of religion or theology, is unsustainable. Oakeshott maintained that the world of concrete or absolute experience is not to be found in any condition independent of our experience. He was unswerving in understanding philosophy as an engagement that arises and ends in human experience. Characterisations of experience in terms of the revelation or the unfolding of a divine or some other super-human purpose are as alien to Oakeshott's writings as proposals that the movement of celestial bodies determines experience. Oakeshott's writings are silent on questions of the existence and character of super-human powers or the relation of God to His creation. [18] They refuse to entertain considerations involving the character of anything beyond human experience.

That Oakeshott was concerned with understanding experience in its own terms and not as a product of some super-human force does little to disqualify consideration of his account of religious experience. Experience in its religious idiom remains for him human experience. Oakeshott's position echoes that of F. H. Bradley who prefaced his treatment of religion with the qualification that:

---

[18] Cp. F.W. Nietzsche, *Human All Too Human*, (Trans. R. J. Hollingdale) (Cambridge, Cambridge University press, 1986), p. 15, Bk I, Sect. 9. 'It is true, there could be a metaphysical world; the absolute possibility of it is hardly to be disputed ... but one can do absolutely nothing with it ... For one could assert nothing at all of the metaphysical world except that it was a being-other...'

> We propose to say nothing of the ultimate truth of religion:
> nothing again of its origin in the world, or in the individual.
> We are to take the religious consciousness as an existing fact,
> and to take it now as we find it in the modern Christian
> mind...'[19]

Religious experience is human not divine experience, even if
claims of divinity are made for what is experienced. This attitude to religious experience is also intimated in Thomas
Hobbes's retort against charges that his rejection of authority
by revelation proved his atheism. Hobbes responded that
doubt in revelation does not equate with doubt in God but is
rather a doubt in the honesty or competency of the individuals
who claimed themselves to be the subject of revelation.[20]
Oakeshott's reference to absolute experience has nothing to do
with positing an absolute beyond human experience or attain-
ing a state where human experience becomes divine. It refers
to the criterion that is implicit in and thus common to all experience; the absolute criterion underlies less coherent worlds of
given experience and more coherent worlds of achieved experience. The absolute begins and ends in experience.

Philosophy is, then, the pursuit of the absolute criterion of
experience by making explicit the presuppositions that are
implied in experience. Oakeshott never stated that the absolute criterion of experience could be realised once and for all in
experience. In fact, he suggested, with varying degrees of
forcefulness, that it could not. At the conclusion of *Experience
and Its Modes* he stated that

> the attempt to find what is completely satisfactory in experi-
> ence is so difficult and dubious an undertaking, leading us so

---

[19]   F.H. Bradley, *Ethical Studies* 2nd Edition, (Oxford, Clarendon Press,
       1927), p. 314.

[20]   T. Hobbes, *Leviathan: Or the Matter, Forme and Power of a Commonwealth
       Ecclesiatical and Civil* (ed. M. Oakeshott) (Oxford, Oxford University
       Press, 1946), Ch. 7, Sect. 7.

far aside from the ways of ordinary thought, that those may be pardoned who prefer the embraces of abstraction.[21]

By the time he published *On Human Conduct* over forty years later, he expressed even less certainty at the possibility of achieving a satisfactory world of unconditional experience in philosophy

> Here, theorizing has revealed itself as an unconditional adventure in which every achievement of understanding is an invitation to investigate itself and where the reports a theorist makes to himself are interim triumphs of temerity over scruple.[22]

The result of being continually *en voyage* in philosophical inquiry could hardly be said to produce a world of experience at all:

> An investigation which denies or questions its own conditions surrenders its opportunity of achieving its own conditional perfection; the theorist who interrogates instead of using his theoretic equipment catches no fish.[23]

Oakeshott never suggested that every world of experience could attain or even should aspire to 'absolute' completeness. A plethora of worlds or modes of abstract experience invite consideration. A world of abstract experience arises when the explication of the presuppositions implicit in a world of given experience is 'arrested' or when the invitation to interrogate presuppositions remains unacknowledged. Although the potential number of arrests and so worlds of experience is so large as to be effectively innumerable, in *Experience and Its*

---

[21] *Experience and Its Modes*, p. 356.

[22] *On Human Conduct*, p. 11. Tariq Modood has suggested that Oakeshott's distancing himself from implying that the absolute was achievable in philosophical reflection is apparent in his description of philosophy as a mode in *The Voice of Poetry*. See 'Oakeshott's Conception of Philosophy'.

[23] *On Human Conduct*, p. 11.

Modes Oakeshott focused upon three. [24] These arrests describe presuppositions about the character of experience upon which are built the worlds of history (the world conceived *sub specie praeteritorum* – the world conceived under the species of past), science (the world conceived *sub specie quantitatis* – the world conceived under the species of quantity) and practice (conduct) (the world conceived *sub specie voluntatis*).

Oakeshott sought to establish the character of the worlds of abstract experience he identified in two regards. First, that they are indeed worlds of experience; that is, that abstract orders of reality and truth follow the general order of experience. This is in keeping with the principle that experience, in all its diverse abstractions, manifests a single principle of coherence. Second, that each of these worlds of abstract experience arises at points where inquiry after the character of experience without qualification has either not commenced or been put to one side. So, a world of abstract experience implies without realising the defining criterion of concrete experience. Each world of abstract experience is undeniably a world of experience but it is not disposed to inquire after the definitive conditions of experience. Worlds of abstract experience imply without realising the definitive criterion of reality.

Like R.G. Collingwood, Oakeshott found in worlds of abstract experience partial views of 'the absolute'. Collingwood argued that

> For religion, God is not one cause but the supreme cause of causes; so for art, beauty is not one concept but the very soul and secret of the world ... To [the artist] beauty is what God is to religion, what truth is to science; it is his 'definition of the Absolute.'[25]

---

[24]   *Experience and Its Modes*, p. 331.

[25]   R G. Collingwood, *Speculum Mentis or the Map of Knowledge*, (Oxford, Clarendon Press, 1924), pp. 66-7.

Each abstract representation of 'the absolute' reflects a world of experience that consists of images that predicate the character of experience on a common set of presuppositions. But while accepting the validity of these representations as worlds of experience, Collingwood and Oakeshott both maintained that they are incapable of achieving that which they imply: *absolute* definition. Worlds of abstract experience rest upon contingent arrests in experience, the arrests occur at points where reality is presupposed to consist in a certain order.

In *Experience and Its Modes* Oakeshott argued that the worlds of philosophical, historical, scientific and practical experience are autonomous each from every other world of experience. He meant by this that an idea or image that belonged to one world of experience would make no sense if its character was mistaken as belonging to another world of experience. So,

> To read the face of big Ben (that is, 'to tell the time') postulates and *therefore* does not question the idea 'time'; 'time' here is unproblematic; the problem is 'what is *the* time?'[26]

To respond to a metaphysical query 'what is time' by answering 'about four post meridian' constitutes a confusion of categories from which no sense can be made.[27] I will not labour Oakeshott's arguments for the autonomy of each of the worlds of experience he identified from the others as they have been made time and again in the secondary literature on his work.

---

[26] *On Human Conduct*, p. 9.

[27] See *Experience and Its Modes*, p. 5, '"Truth", says Bacon, "comes more easily out of error than of confusions": but the view which I have to recommend is that confusion, *ignoratio elenchi*, is itself the most fatal of all errors, and that it occurs whenever argument or inference passes from one world of experience to another...'

2. The Character of the World
Conceived as a Species of Will

In conduct we do not realise concrete reality understood as the defining criterion of experience without further qualification. In acknowledging this circumstance, it is reasonable to inquire after Oakeshott's characterisation of the world of experience that arises in the conduct of life and how this order of experience falls short of the absolute. The world of conduct 'calls first our attention ... as desire and aversion...'[28] However, it

> comprises far more than is ordinarily attributed to it. It comprises all that we mean by a 'moral' life, a life directed by an idea of the right and the good; it includes all that we mean by beauty; it comprises the religious life...[29]

I shall explore Oakeshott's account of the distinctive qualities of various types of identities within the world of conduct such as desire, moral judgement, religious experience and poetic appreciation in subsequent chapters. The present section focuses upon the world of conduct, not in terms of the characteristics that distinguish each of these types of activity from the others, but in terms of their belonging to a common world of experience – the qualities that they share.

Oakeshott argued that the world of conduct, like every world of experience, consists of images and ideas that imply a common presupposition about the character of experience. The cardinal presupposition implied in moral images of approbation and disapprobation and prudential images of desire and aversion is change. Change is also a characteristic of other worlds of experience such as the explanatory worlds of science, history and philosophy and we must be clear about the specific character of change that Oakeshott attributed to

---

[28] M. Oakeshott, *Rationalism in Politics and Other Essays* (ed. T. Fuller) (Indianapolis, Liberty Press, 1991), pp. 497–8.

[29] *Experience and Its Modes*, p. 296.

the world of conduct. He distinguished change in the other worlds of experience that he considered in *Experience and Its Modes* from change in the world of conduct observing that

> Scientific and historical experience involve processes of abandoning truths which were never true in search of a coherent world of facts; practice involves a process in which the achievement of a coherent world of facts is merely preliminary to its transformation.[30]

Worlds of historical and scientific experience change as new facts supersede established beliefs and are, in turn, themselves superseded. The character of change in these worlds of theoretical experience is incidental to them. In changing their truth claims historians and scientists alter them (provisionally) for all time. When, for instance, what was thought to be an authentic historical fact is discovered to be a forgery, it is realised to have been a forgery for all time. When Copernicus proposed that the Earth was not at the centre of the Universe but in orbit around the Sun, he was suggesting that it had never been at the centre of the Universe. If Copernicus's new regime of cycles and epicycles that described the motions of celestial bodies was true, it was true for all time. Truth is unchanging in both of the above instances; something that is discovered to be untrue was always untrue. So, change in the worlds of historical and scientific experience occurs, but it is incidental to the truth claims that these worlds of experience make about reality.

Change in the world of conduct is intrinsic to its character as a distinctive world of experience. In the world of conduct, every identity, event and thing necessarily presupposes its own passing:

> Mortality, I take it, is the central fact of practical existence; death is the central fact of life. I do not, of course, mean merely

---

[30]   *Ibid.*, p. 267.

> human mortality, the fact that we must one day cease to be; I
> mean the far more devastating mortality ... of pleasures and
> pains, desires, achievements, emotions and affections.[31]

In the world of conduct truth is itself a changing entity; 'Here
and here only, can what was true yesterday be false today' and
may be so without contradiction.[32] The utterance 'I am poor' is
not a claim for all time. It is a declaration of an undesirable situation and is significant only if things could have been or
could be different and the utterance refers to a situation that
may be altered in any number of ways.[33]

Oakeshott argued that the brute fact of change underlying
and infecting every identity in the world of conduct arises in
the presupposition that reality consists of not one but two
worlds of experience; a world of 'what is now' and a world of
'what ought to be'. The worlds of 'what is' and 'what ought to
be' are discrepant but inseparable from one another. Every
image of desire or moral judgement presupposes a world of
'what ought to be' that is discrepant from 'what is now'. The
worlds of 'what is' and 'what ought to be' are inseparable from
one another but each is also destructive of the other.[34] The

---

[31] *Ibid.*, p. 273.

[32] *Ibid.*, p. 267.

[33] See *On Human Conduct*, pp. 41–4, 'Understanding his situation as that of
being in debt and finding this unacceptable, Z recognises himself to be
invited to respond in an action or an utterance ... [He] may decide to
offer to pay a bit on account, but how much? and which of the ways of
raising the instalment shall he choose to explore? and exactly how shall
he pay over the sum decided upon? ... He may consider marrying an
heiress, pawning his violin, missing dinner for a month or going into
voluntary liquidation. He may try to reassure his creditors in any of the
ways which he thinks them likely to be reassured. Or he may consider
escaping from them in any of the many ways in which a man may
attempt such an escape – feigning death, emigrating to Nicaragua, join-
ing the Foreign Legion, or disguising himself and taking a job under an
assumed name with the Yeovil Town Council.'

[34] Cf. P. de Man, 'Literary History and Literary Modernity' in *Blindness and
Insight: Essays in the Rhetoric of Contemporary Criticism*, (2nd edition)

complete overcoming of one world by the other would remove the condition, the presupposition, which makes it sensible to speak of an act of will or an object willed.

There is nothing new in Oakeshott's presentation of the world of conduct as a world of experience that presupposes the transience of particular desires and approvals. This idea has been portrayed nowhere more dramatically than in Hobbes's definition of worldly felicity as

> *Continual success* in obtaining those things which a man from time to time desireth ... For there is no perpetual tranquility of mind, while we live here; because life is motion and can never be without desire...[35]

The satisfaction of a desire never signals the end of desiring. At best it provides a temporary respite from desire in the enjoyment of a present condition before a new desire arises to usurp contentment. Often the satisfaction of a desire merely realises a condition that must be secured against further, undesirable change and resistance to change is an exhibition of will that seeks change by confounding what would otherwise be.[36] Even suicide, an act in which the self seeks the ultimate release from its world of interminable change is still a way of conduct *in* life.[37]

Thus, the fundamental presupposition underlying the world in which we live is mutability. Mutability is the essence

(London, Routledge, 1989) and, by the same author, 'What is Modern?' in *Critical Writings 1953–1978*, (ed. L. Waters) (Minneapolis, University of Minnesota Press, 1989).

[35] Hobbes, *Leviathan*, Ch. 6, Sect. 17, p. 39.

[36] *Experience and Its Modes,* pp. 257–8, 'To maintain is always to change. There is here, as everywhere in practical activity, an unrealized idea, an unfulfilled desire, a "to be" discrepant from "what is".'

[37] *Ibid.*, p. 257, 'He who determines to do away with his life is no less conducting his life than the man who spends it in satisfying his ambitions: and the man who seeks satisfaction in imagination or devotion to God requires to be no less active than he who looks for it in conquest or an empire.'

of each moment as well as its nemesis and every image belonging to this world is infected with change. Yet to speak of willing, desiring and approving assumes an identifiable individual who wills, desires and approves. It is not clear, however, how an individual could be constituted or constitute itself under circumstances so hostile to identity. Oakeshott argued that the principle on which individuality is based in the world of conduct is separateness:

> the principle on which practical thinking establishes its conception of the self is a principle of separation or distinction … The self, in practical experience, is what is separate, unique and self-contained.[38]

A self conceived as will is an identity that understands itself in terms of its otherness from the world in which it exists, that is, a world of other individuals and things on which to act. This self can only be understood and understand itself through its capacity to divorce itself from that which provides the conditions of its existence.

Oakeshott's account of individuality as a principle of separateness is distinct from his account of philosophical individuality, which he defined in terms of completeness. The criterion of individuality as separateness is symptomatic of the abstract character of the world to which it belongs – an individual conceived in terms of separateness could never achieve completeness, because it presupposes something from which it is separate. An individual that secured complete separation from its world would cease to be of that world – it would renounce the very reality that it seeks to achieve in securing its individuality. This is to say no more than that individuals conceived in terms of will presuppose their abstract (incomplete) character. Their abstract character is reflected in their ability to

---

[38]   *Ibid.*, p. 269.

separate themselves, albeit incompletely, from the world of other individuals.

A succinct summary of the incoherent character of individuality conceived in terms of separateness is provided by R. L. Nettleship:

> for everything except the absolute, individuality implies limitation (i.e. environment), and the great differences in the associations which the word [individuality] has seems to come from the double fact that, while every individuality is measured by the amount which it holds together (i.e. by the amount of what would otherwise be environment that it converts into itself), it is also measured *against* what still remains environment, what it excludes, [what it] asserts itself against.[39]

Nettleship's 'double fact of individuality' reveals an abstract individuality conceived in terms of separateness which can be neither absolutely complete but nor is it nothing. From the standpoint of the absolute defining criterion of experience, this type of individuality is abstract because it presupposes its incompleteness. However, the inevitable incompleteness of individuality as separateness does not preclude more and less adequate achievements of identity in the world of conduct. Nettleship concluded his remarks on individuality by observing that:

> The difficulty is to keep between the two extremes, as Aristotle might say, that of being nothing because one has only *one* centre, and that of being nothing because one has *no* centre; death by stagnation and death by dissipation ... Practically the important thing seems to be that one should try to be the *growing* centre of a *growing* circumference, so that while one is always ready to change one's individuality without fear of

---

[39] Nettleship, *Philosophical Remains*, p. 35.

losing it, one should always carry the individuality that one has so far made into each new environment ...[40]

Nettleship did not explore how individuality might be carried into each new environment and, indeed, how this individuality might be established in the first place.[41] Oakeshott recognised the extremes of conduct in much the same terms as Nettleship although he insisted that the extremes of conduct remained within its bounds – *being* nothing is still a condition of being. However, he devoted considerable effort to characterising various postulates in terms of which selves establish themselves as identities in conduct.

3. The Substantive and Formal Aspects of Conduct

A fleeting reflection of Nettleship's extremes of conduct can be found in Oakeshott's account of conduct in the first essay of *On Human Conduct*, 'On the Theoretical Understanding of Human Conduct'. He described the limits of conduct as, on the one hand,

> an agent doing nothing because all the actions he can think of seem to carry with them unacceptabilities greater than that which he now suffers; and ... [on the other,] an agent considering the sovereign release from all unacceptable situations, namely, suicide.[42]

Of course, an agent choosing to do nothing in relation to a specific situation in which they find themselves does not preclude action in other situations. However, if an agent were to choose to do absolutely nothing because of a belief that any action car-

---

[40] *Ibid.*, pp. 37–8.

[41] Nettleship is notorious for not having published much. See A.C. Bradley's 'Biographical Sketch' at the beginning of Nettleship's *Philosophical Remains*.

[42] *On Human Conduct*, p. 43.

ried with it greater unacceptabilities than those currently suffered, it would denote as close to a stagnant condition as one could obtain in conduct. In this circumstance, the only agency exhibited by an agent is the monotonous choice not to act. The dissipation of an agent that follows the choice to suicide needs no further exposition.[43]

Between the extremes of stagnation and dissipation, Oakeshott observed the 'eligible alternatives in conduct are virtually unlimited ...'[44] The remaining chapters address Oakeshott's characterisations of some of the ways in which, in an order of experience so hostile to individuality, selves might avail themselves of opportunities to establish themselves as appropriately ordered identities. Before commencing direct consideration of these various manners of establishing and maintaining identity, I will briefly lay some groundwork by outlining Oakeshott's characterisation of conduct in terms of two postulates that he identified underlying this order of experience. These postulates can be used as a basis for reflecting upon Oakeshott's account of the responses that moderns have made in seeking to realise the good life. His account of conduct is not confined to the postulates on which the following section focuses, but it is these characteristics that go to the heart of the current study.

---

[43] That the choice to suicide is an exhibition of agency and thus falls within the world of conduct, and that this choice constitutes an extremity of conduct, is evident in the strength of response it has provoked from many who have commented on the moral character this choice reflects. For instance, G.K. Chesterton: 'The man who kills himself, kills all men; as far as he is concerned he wipes out the world. His act is worse ... than any rape or dynamite outrage. For it destroys all buildings: it insults all women. The thief is satisfied with diamonds; but the suicide is not: that is his crime ... The thief compliments the things he steals, if not the owner of them. But the suicide insults everything on earth by not stealing it. He defies every flower by refusing to live for its sake. There is not a tiny creature in the cosmos at which his death is not a sneer.' *Orthodoxy*, (London, Bodley Head, 1957), pp. 115–6.

[44] *On Human Conduct*, p. 44.

The first postulate underlying conduct identified by Oakeshott that is of significance to the current exercise refers to the substantive performances that an agent chooses in seeking wished for outcomes. Substantive performances are made by agents responding to what they understand as specific unacceptabilities in their situation and who by the performance seek new situations in which the unacceptability is removed.[45] The substantive performances of an agent are attempts to realise substantive conditions that are imagined to be more desirable than their current situation. The second postulate underlying conduct refers to the formal practices that qualify without specifying the performances that an agent might choose in seeking wished for substantive outcomes:

> what joins agents in conduct [and] is to be recognized as a 'practice' ... is a prudential or a moral adverbial qualification of choices and performances ... in which conduct is understood in terms of a procedure.[46]

A practice qualifies performances so that

> Words such as punctually, considerately, civilly, scientifically, legally, candidly, judicially, poetically, morally, etc., do not specify performances; they postulate performances and specify procedural conditions to be taken into account when choosing and acting.[47]

Substantive performances and formal practices are distinct but inseparable postulates of conduct. Substantive performances that had no reference to a practice would have no significance. Even a baby's cry or an infant's demand 'I want' is understood as a subscription to a rude prudential practice indicating a noticed unacceptability and a wished for satisfaction – feed me. And without substantive performances there

---

[45]   *Ibid.*, p. 41.

[46]   *Ibid.*, p. 55.

[47]   *Ibid.*, pp. 55–6.

would be no practices; 'Practices are themselves the outcomes of performances.'[48] Practices may be explicitly established or modified or dissolved by a performance, for example, in the enactment of a law or the adoption of a rule. But practices are subject to continual modification by the performances they qualify. A practice

> emerges as a continuously invented and always unfinished by-product of performances related to the achievement of imagined and wished-for satisfactions other than that of having a procedure, and it becomes recognizable when it has acquired a certain degree of definition and authority or acknowledged utility.[49]

Substantive performances and formal practices imply other postulates such as free agents whose choices of performances in acknowledging practices are themselves exhibitions of intelligence, however, it is the substantive and formal aspects of conduct that provide one of the threads through the following work. Oakeshott found in every action a performance that is also a subscription to a practice. Conduct always has a substantive and a formal element. It is my contention that Oakeshott's characterisation of moral characters, modes of association and their religious and poetic analogues that understand conduct as primarily the pursuit of substantive conditions does not provide a strong basis for maintaining identity in the face of the mutability that is presupposed in the world of conduct. And moral characters, modes of association and their religious and poetic analogues that understand conduct as the subscription to formal practices, while subject to the mutability that is presupposed in the world of conduct, provide some reprieve from its inevitability in which identity might be established and maintained.

[48] *Ibid.*, p. 56.
[49] *Ibid.*

Chapter 3

Religion, the World and the Self

The following chapter sets out Oakeshott's account of the appropriate order in terms of which a self may seek to establish itself as a moral identity; the second area of moral consideration identified by Lewis. Oakeshott exhibited a keen sense of the historicity of the moral practices, dispositions and characters that give shape and colour to his account of the self. These practices, dispositions and characters emerged in a set of contingent circumstances that he called 'modern Europe'. The contingency of the event under consideration means that an exploration of Oakeshott's conception of self provides not a recommendation or prescription of what a self ought to be but a description of the practices, dispositions and characters that have emerged over time in response to a particular situation. However, neither is the historical character of the self sketched by Oakeshott an admission of cultural or moral relativism. Rather it is a conception of self that acknowledges the peculiar circumstances of modern Europe. It recognises that moderns have conceived of the self in peculiarly modern ways.

1. The Morality of the Individual and the Morality of the Anti-Individual

Through the 1950s, '60s and '70s Oakeshott set out the character of the self in modern Europe in terms of two characters, which he called 'the individual' and 'the anti-individual'. He first formulated these characters in an essay entitled '*Die Massen in der repräsentativen Demokratie*', which was published in 1957 and subsequently appeared in English as 'The Masses in Representative Democracy' in 1961.[1] The individual and the anti-individual are also mentioned in the posthumously published *Harvard Lectures* delivered in 1958 and re-appear one last time in the final essay of *On Human Conduct*, 'On the Character of a Modern European State'. These essays are all historical works.[2] The disposition to be an individual and its subsequent expression in terms of moral approval is, for Oakeshott, an historical rather than a 'natural' or teleological fact.[3] So far as Oakeshott was concerned, there is no human nature or natural individual ready to enter upon the historical

---

[1]   'Die Massen in der repräsentativen Demokratie', *Masse und Demokratie*, (ed. A. Hunold) (Erlenbach-Zürich und Stuttgart, Rentsch, 1957). 'The Masses in Representative Democracy' in *Freedom and Serfdom: An Anthology of Western Thought* (ed. A. Hunold) (Dordrecht, D. Reidel Publishing, 1961). This essay is re-published in the Fuller edition of *Rationalism in Politics* to which I shall refer.

[2]   Although, whether or not these essays realise Oakeshott's own criterion as to what constitutes good historical practice has been contested. See D. Boucher, 'Politics in a Different Mode: An Appreciation of Michael Oakeshott 1901–1990', *History of Political Thought*, 12 (4) (Winter, 1991), p. 728, 'Oakeshott's 'accounts of the rise of the individual are caricatures of the transformations which Michelet and Burkhardt tried to capture in their accounts … and certainly fall short of subscription to the postulates of history as Oakeshott himself identified them.' Oakeshott acknowledged that he may have stretched some events and characters to make his point in 'On the Character of a Modern European State'. See M. Oakeshott, 'On Misunderstanding Human Conduct: A Reply to My Critics', *Political Theory*, 4 (3), (August, 1976), pp. 359–60.

[3]   See *Rationalism in Politics*, p. 370, 'Human individuality is an historical emergence, as "artificial" and as "natural" as the landscape.'

stage and there is no pre-ordained historical *telos* declaring the
necessity or even the desirability that individuality be finally
realised in its modern European shape. The individual is an
historical event whose 'necessity' can be established only after
the fact. Oakeshott understood historical events as arising in
contingent occurrences; they are not teleological necessities. A
morality in which individuality is not the central focus is, then,
neither 'unhistorical' nor is it necessarily the expression of a
'less developed' phase of European history and it is certainly
not an outrage against 'human nature'. The truth of the historical emergence of the individual is unique to this particular
event and thus cannot be used as a template to construct a
Weltgeist or to measure the 'progressivencss' of other historical
occurrences.[4]

Oakeshott followed Jacob Burkhardt, 'who may still be recognized as its most perceptive historian', in finding that the
modern European individual emerged in thirteenth century
Italy.[5] Understanding the emergence of the individual and
more generally the advent of modern Europe entails understanding some of the features of the medieval world out of
which this character arose. And it should be apparent that
Oakeshott's understanding of the event 'medieval world' is
neither a Marxian stage in the development of productive
forces nor can it be measured in terms of utilitarian degrees of
'Happiness' or 'Democracy'.[6] Rather, Oakeshott understood
the medieval world hermeneutically by discovering the terms

---

[4]   In *Experience and its Modes* Oakeshott identified uniqueness as a presup-
      position underlying the conception of individuality in the world of his-
      torical experience.

[5]   *On Human Conduct*, p. 240 and *Rationalism in Politics*, p. 365.

[6]   See *On Human Conduct*, p. 242, 'The contraction [of the rise of the modern
      European individual] into a history of so-called "bourgeois market-
      society capitalism" is a notorious botch. Of course, this disposition [to be
      an individual] displayed itself in commerce. But anyone who believes
      that Frère Jean Entommeurs or Parini were "possessive individualists"
      … is capable of believing anything.'

in which it understood itself. He began his account by describing the character of the moral beliefs out of which the individual emerged. He called this medieval morality 'the morality of communal ties'.[7] The distinctive features of the medieval moral outlook are evident throughout the society that they shaped:

> Not only were ordinary activities, those concerned with getting a living, communal in character, but so also were decisions, rights and responsibilities. Relationships and allegiances normally sprang from status and rarely extricated themselves from the analogy of kinship. For the most part anonymity prevailed ... What differentiated one man from another was insignificant when compared with what was enjoyed in common as a group of some sort.[8]

Although the morality of communal ties lacked a conception of individuality in its modern sense, it is not a condition in which life should be thought of as stunted or undeveloped. The medieval world was not a Dark or Middle Age before a Renaissance and Enlightenment. Indicting medieval life on the grounds that it lacked individuality implies that individuality is a universal measure and, on Oakeshott's view, this sort of contrivance is inappropriate to history. In contrast to the sort of view that understands medieval life in terms of a world of modern values, Oakeshott acknowledged that the medieval period projected a particular vitality of its own which in some ways only intimated what was to come but in others surpassed modern achievements.[9]

---

[7]   *Rationalism in Politics*, p. 372.

[8]   *Ibid.*, p. 365.

[9]   Cf. Collingwood's observation that 'The men of the middle ages, as we look back on them now, appear as half children and half giants. In the narrowness of their outlook, the smallness of the problems they faced, their fanciful and innocent superstition, their combination of qualities which a reflective or critical society would find intolerably contradictory, they are children, and it is difficult for us to believe that human

In his description of the decline of the medieval world, Oakeshott was not inquiring after the causes of the break-down of medieval communal life and the demise of the morality of communal ties but rather the change in self-understanding that accompanied it. The breakdown of the medieval world and the subsequent loosening of communal ties are contributing factors to, as well as results of, the emergence of the new disposition to be an individual. At different times and in different regions of Europe the disposition to be an individual touched all levels and walks of life.[10] Oakeshott's individual 'was not generated in claims and assertions on behalf of individuality, but in sporadic divergences' from the morality of communal ties.[11] There was no prior body of moral beliefs approving of this condition let alone general principles from which to derive claims and rights to individual self-determination; all this came later. Individuality had first to become known in practice before this experience could be morally approved of or its postulates explored at a theoretical level. Individuals were individuals not in terms of their adherence to, or their profession of a particular moral doctrine but simply on account of their disposition to make choices for themselves.

----

beings could be so simple. But in the solid magnitude of their achievements, their systems of law and philosophy, their creation and organization of huge nation-states, their incredible cathedrals, and above all their gradual forging of a civilized world out of a chaos of barbarism, they seemed possessed with a tenacity and a vastness of purpose that we can only call gigantic. They seem to be tiny people doing gigantic things.' *Speculum Mentis*, pp. 23–4.

[10] *On Human Conduct*, p. 239. 'It displayed itself in the persons of younger sons making their own way in a world which had little place for them, of foot-loose adventurers who left the land to take trade, of town-dwellers who had emancipated themselves from the communal ties of the countryside, of vagabond scholars, in the speculative audacities of Abelard, in venturesome heresy, in the lives of intrepid boys and men who left home to seek their fortunes each intent upon living a life for "a man like me", and in the relationships of men and women.'

[11] *Rationalism in Politics*, p. 365.

The individual was not, however, the only character to step upon Oakeshott's late-medieval, early-modern European stage. Another character also emerged from the gradual disintegration of the morality of communal ties

> in a world being transformed by the aspirations and activities of those who were excited by these opportunities, there were some people, by circumstance or by temperament, less ready than others to respond to this invitation; and for many the invitation to make choices came before the ability to make them and was consequently recognized as a burden.'[12]

Oakeshott called this character the 'individual *manqué*'. Each of the terms, 'individual' and '*manqué*', notices a defining quality of this character. First, the individual *manqué* is an individual; it is a character that appeared only when the hold of the morality of communal ties upon European self-understanding had been sufficiently weakened. So, the individual *manqué* belongs to the modern world of the individual rather than the medieval world of communal ties.[13] But, second, the individual *manqué* is incapable of realising itself as an individual. Thus, Oakeshott distinguished this character from the individual as only a potential or unfulfilled individual. The individual *manqué* is distinct from the individual, not in terms of the historical epoch to which it belongs, but in terms of its incapacity to realise what it actually is.

Oakeshott's historical sketch of the emergence of the individual goes on to describe the departure of the last vestiges of the morality of communal ties that still exerted a hold over many areas of life well into the sixteenth century. The individual consolidated its achievements in a 'morality of the individual': 'from the experience of individuality there sprang, in the course of time, a morality appropriate to it – a disposition not

---

[12]   *Ibid.*, pp. 370–1.

[13]   *Ibid.*, p. 371, 'this individual *manqué* was not a relic of a past age; he was a 'modern' character …'

only to explore individuality but to approve of the pursuit of individuality.'[14] This consolidation of the character of the individual in a body of moral beliefs 'constituted a considerable moral revolution ... [it] swept aside the morality appropriate to the defunct communal order, but left little room for any alternative to *itself*.'[15] The moral revolution to which Oakeshott referred is most apparent, however, not in the success of the individual consolidated in a moral disposition, but in the transformation of the character of the individual *manqué*:

> Already outmanoeuvred in the field (in conduct) he now suffered a defeat at home, in his own character. What had been no more than a doubt about his ability to hold his own in a struggle for existence, became a radical self-distrust; what had been merely a hostile prospect, disclosed itself as an abyss; what had been the discomfort of ill-success was turned into the misery of guilt.[16]

The potential individual was forced to confront what it had hitherto been able to avoid (its individuality) and, in this confrontation, what had remained until this point mere potential was pressed into action. This action is manifest, however, not as a movement towards realising the individuality that acted as its impetus, but in revolt against the morality of the individual. This revolt took the form of

> envy, jealousy and resentment ... a new disposition was generated: the impulse to escape from the predicament by imposing it upon all mankind. From the frustrated 'individual *manqué*' there sprang the militant 'anti-individual', disposed to assimilate the world to his own character by deposing the individual and destroying his moral prestige.[17]

---

[14] *Ibid.*, p. 372.

[15] *Ibid.*

[16] *Ibid.*

[17] *Ibid.*

The individual *manqué* had occupied a situation that was perceived as unsatisfactory but bearable. With the 'complete' victory of the individual, expressed in a morality that approved of this condition, the situation of the individual *manqué* became intolerable and this intolerable situation generated a 'morality of the anti-individual'.

The outcome is two moral systems each justifying and approving different conceptions of the human condition. The first posits:

> a reading of the human condition in which the race of men is recognized to be saddled with an unsought and inescapable "freedom" which in some respects they are ill-equipped to exercise; namely, the recognition of this condition as the emblem of human dignity and as a condition for each individual to explore, to cultivate, to make the most of and to enjoy as an opportunity rather than suffer as a burden.[18]

The morality of the individual approves of a condition which is far from a withdrawn hedonistic solipsism of selfishness:

> nowhere is this seen more clearly than in the writings of Kant. Every human being, in virtue of not being subject to natural necessity is recognized ... to be a Person, an end in himself, absolute and autonomous.[19]

A morality of the individual requires that individuals acknowledge and approve of the condition of individuality, not only in themselves but in others.

The second type of moral system that Oakeshott identified arises as a response to the morality of the individual. This morality is 'intolerant not only of superiority but of difference, [it is] disposed to allow in all others only a replica of [the anti-individual] and [it] unite[s him] with his fellows in a

---

[18]   *On Human Conduct*, p. 236.
[19]   *Rationalism in Politics*, p. 367.

revulsion from distinctness.'[20] The morality of the anti-individual is so opposed to the idea of individual determination that what is deemed the vice of self-love 'was to be replaced, not by love of "others", or by "charity" or by "benevolence" (which would have entailed a relapse into the vocabulary of individuality), but by the love of the community.'[21] The morality of the anti-individual, like the morality of the individual, arises out of and qualifies conduct between individuals. It opposes the idea of relations between individuals, however, by promoting a higher entity (the community) over these relationships, so that relationships occur not between individuals but rather between an individual and a 'higher' entity or purpose. Individuals are thus not deemed responsible to themselves or to one another but to this 'higher' purpose to which all are equally subordinate.

Oakeshott's most concerted exploration of the morality of the individual and the morality of the anti-individual occurs in terms of their conceptions of the proper office of government. The morality of the individual requires a government in which 'every subject was secured of the right to pursue his chosen directions of activity as little hindered as might be by his fellows or by the exactions of government itself, and as little distracted by communal pressures.'[22] It requires a government strong enough to protect the rights of individuals but not strong enough to pose a new threat to these rights. The morality of the anti-individual conceives of the office of government in very different terms:

> To govern was understood to be the exercise of power in order to impose and maintain the substantive condition of human circumstance identified as 'the public good'; to be governed

[20]   *On Human Conduct*, p. 278.

[21]   *Rationalism in Politics*, p. 375.

[22]   *Ibid.*, p. 369.

was, for the 'anti-individual', to have made for him the choices
he was unable to make for himself.[23]

The morality of the anti-individual understands the role of
government as settling a single desirable condition of human
community and then ensuring that there is no deviation from
this condition.

Oakeshott explored the morality of the individual and the
morality of the anti-individual in terms of their conceptions of
the proper office of government in detail on a number of occasions. I shall consider these accounts at greater length in the
next chapter. His attendance upon the proper office of government as conceived by the individual and the anti-individual
has encouraged a view among commentators that the primary
significance of these characters is political. I am suggesting,
however, that these characters are more than mere political
emblems. Each conveys a conception of self that intimates a
distinct idea of salvation and damnation as well as the appropriate terms in which selves associate with others, and each
generates a distinct view of the general purpose of life – what
we are made for. In short, if Oakeshott's response to each of the
moral categories identified by Lewis is sought, the appropriate starting place is his characterisation of the individual and
the anti-individual.

The individual and the anti-individual are, then, central to
Oakeshott's account of moral experience as it emerged in
modern Europe. However, many of the earlier works in which
he considered the character of the self and the state were composed before he identified the individual and the anti-individual as moral characters. Nevertheless, they can be glimpsed
standing in the wings of these works. At any rate, the lack of

---

[23] *Ibid.*, p. 377.

explicit connections drawn by Oakeshott between the individual and the anti-individual and other subjects that he considered does not preclude his readers tracing for themselves the outlines of and implications for these characters in these works.

2. Salvation: Religion or the World

Oakeshott's most comprehensive considerations of the appropriate terms in which modern selves are constituted can be found in his writings on religious experience. In religious experience a self reflects upon and responds to its relation to eternity – its status understood as a category of eternity. The language of religious experience occurs beyond the mundane desires, approvals, aversions and disapprobations of selves living their day-to-day lives and refers to salvation and damnation – whether and in what manner a self is saved or lost. Before continuing it is appropriate at this point to revisit some comments I made on considering Oakeshott's metaphysics. There I stated that Oakeshott's writings do not speculate on the character of God and eternity or of the relation of the temporal to the eternal. Eternity is beyond human experience and thus out of the bounds of Oakeshott's considerations. Once again then, the issue arises of what sense it makes to refer to Oakeshott's conception of religious experience understood in the terms just outlined.

An element of the sense in which I am referring to categories such as eternity, salvation and damnation in Oakeshott's work is captured in the concluding passage of a talk presented at the International Philosophy, Science and Theology Festival by the former Primus of the Scottish Episcopal Church and Bishop of Edinburgh, Richard Holloway. Holloway recalled

> Lewis's encounter … with an American doctoral student who asked him about faith, and 'What if it was proved to be wrong?

That there wasn't anything to which it corresponded.' And Lewis shouted back, 'Why then, you would have paid the universe a compliment it doesn't deserve!'

The Bishop concluded in an appositely Oakeshottian vein by citing the quixotic verse of the twentieth century Basque philosopher, Miguel de Unamuno: 'Man is perishing, that may be, but if it is nothingness that awaits, then let us live so that it will be an unjust fate.'[24] The debate about the existence and character of God and eternity and their relation to life can be put to one side without disallowing consideration of what could be meant for a self to live its life as if eternity were at stake.

Oakeshott's early references to religion bear all the hallmarks of the same intellectual tradition that influenced his writings on metaphysics at this time. They reflect the approach and style of the British Idealists.[25] The British Idealists generally agreed that religious experience describes a completion in experience.[26] However, Oakeshott's inheritance of the Idealist account of absolute experience and truth as principles of completion and coherence raises as many questions for his characterisation of religion as it settles. In particular, the issue is raised of the relation of God to the absolute and the relation of the world of conduct (in which individuality is understood as separateness) to the world of philosophical experience (in which individuality is understood as completion).

---

[24] R. Holloway, 'Inns on Roads', broadcast 22 July 2001 by Australian Broadcasting Commission programme Encounter. Transcript available at http://www.abc.net.au/rn/relig/enc/stories/s445746.htm

[25] In Oakeshott's concluding footnote to his pamphlet, 'Religion and the Moral Life' he states 'Those who are acquainted with his writings, will recognize how much I am indebted to F.H. Bradley throughout this discussion.' *Religion, Politics and the Moral Life*, p. 45 He also refers to Bosanquet, p. 41.

[26] For an excellent overview of the Hegelian conceptions of religion in Britain (particularly T.H. Green) that preceded Oakeshott's understanding see A. Vincent and R. Plant, *Philosophy, Politics and Citizenship: The Life and Thought of the British Idealists*, (Oxford, Basil Blackwell, 1984), Ch. 2.

Taking a particular example of the Idealist position on religion may provide a clearer picture of the issue at hand. R.G. Collingwood argued that Christianity represents the highest achievement in religious experience because the image of Christ unifies in one person the sin of individual separation from God (Christ's nature as man) with the occasion of his redemption to the divine (his nature as God).[27] In Collingwood's Christ, then, we find the two criteria of individuality observed in Oakeshott's characterisations of the world conceived *sub specie voluntatis* (separateness) and the world conceived *sub specie aeternitatis* (completeness). The dual nature of Christ, His nature as both man and God, is an article of faith for Christians. However, for the philosopher to rest on this account invites a modal confusion of the same order as answering a query 'what is time?' with the statement 'about four pm'. We must be clear on the modal character of individuality in religious experience so as to establish whether it has anything to offer a self seeking identity in conduct. If it is found that religion conceives of individuality as completeness rather than separateness it would appear to be categorially irrelevant to conduct. Practically, religious experience would be useless.

In his earliest substantial publication on religion, 'Religion and the Moral Life', Oakeshott identified religious experience as belonging unambiguously to the world of conduct that is constituted in terms of abstract identities of desire and moral approval; identities that presuppose their own passing and incompleteness. He denounced the view that religion is outside the world of moral conduct as 'abstract and extrava-

---

[27] Collingwood, *Speculum Mentis*, p. 139, see also pp. 142–3 and 302. Collingwood does not specify with which religions he is comparing Christianity but one may assume he has in mind other world religions like Hinduism, Buddhism, Judaism and Islam.

gant.'[28] The problem confronting Oakeshott, then, is the sense in which religious experience constitutes completion when it inhabits a world of experience that presupposes reality as interminable change and takes as its principle of identity the separateness of an individual from its world.

In 'Religion and the Moral Life' the character of moral achievement clearly suffers interminable change that infects all achievement in the world of conduct: 'out of every moral success the further 'ought' springs up to condemn you once more: it is a series without an end.'[29] Viewed from the principle of individuality the interminable series of oughts in moral conduct defeats any attempt by a self to realise completion in experience. Oakeshott went on to argue, however, that in religion the inevitable incompleteness of morality is resolved: 'What in morality was a mere "should be", in religion becomes an "is."'[30] In religious experience the moral self is completed by overcoming the assertion of its identity as a principle of separateness; 'In religion, we achieve goodness, not by becoming better, but by losing ourselves in God.'[31] Striving to be better presupposes a self that only ever approaches the good. It is only by giving up the effort to be good and acquiescing in what might be called the grace of God that the good is no longer separate from the self, and thus the self finds completion.

Oakeshott's presentation of religious experience as achieving a completion where moral conduct presupposes incom-

---

[28] *Religion, Politics and the Moral Life*, p. 39. Cp. Bradley, *Ethical Studies*, pp. 314–5, 'A man who is religious and does not act morally, is an impostor, or his religion is a false one ... Religion is essentially a doing and a doing which is moral.'

[29] *Religion, Politics and the Moral Life*, p. 41. Cf. Bradley, *Ethical Studies*, p. 313, 'Morality is an endless process, and therefore a self-contradiction; and being such, it does not remain standing in itself, but feels the impulse to transcend its existing reality.'

[30] *Religion, Politics and the Moral Life*, p. 42.

[31] *Ibid.*

pleteness does little more than assert the principle of 'what is' over the principle of 'what ought to be'. This characterisation of religion has many precedents where greater or truer reality is found in God's love than in the illusion of worldly affairs or the glamour of evil. However, it does little to unravel the problem that Oakeshott inherited from the Idealists, namely how can religious experience be understood as a completion when it belongs within the world of conduct with its presupposition of experience as change and separateness. How can an identity subsist within the world of conduct without presupposing both the world of 'what is' and the world of 'what ought to be'? It would appear that either religion must transform the character of the world of conduct or suffer defeat and acquiesce in this world. In 'Religion and the Moral Life' religion appears to compromise Oakeshott's strict insistence on the modal identity of experience.

Six years after the publication of 'Religion and the Moral Life', Oakeshott re-iterated the character of religion as completion within the world of conduct in *Experience and Its Modes*. He argued that religious experience is not the occasion of a theoretical transformation of a less coherent world of experience into a more coherent world; rather in religion we find 'practical life in its most concrete mood …'[32] Religion is not logically or qualitatively more complete than other activities in the world of conduct; it 'differs from other forms of practical activity, not in kind, but in degree …'[33] A self lives religiously 'whenever the seriousness with which we embrace this enterprise of achieving a coherent world of practical ideas reaches a certain strength and intensity …'[34] The idea of salvation in life, of a life that achieves some sort of consummation is here less strongly opposed to Oakeshott's account of the ever-changing

[32] *Experience and Its Modes,* p. 295.

[33] *Ibid.*

[34] *Ibid.*

character of the world of conduct than was previously the case. Religious experience arises in the seriousness and intensity of the enterprise to gain completeness in life. However, qualifying the characterisation of religious experience as arising in the attempt rather than in the achievement of completion raises questions of why an exercise so obviously doomed to failure might be undertaken or even contemplated in the first place.

In conduct, a world of 'what is' always supposes a discrepant world of 'what ought to be'. While both worlds exist, life can never be complete; but without both worlds, the world of conduct breaks down altogether because each world implies the other, each is understood in terms of the other. The attainment of completeness in life, 'salvation' to invoke the religious idiom, must involve either one of two (apparently impossible) alternatives. Either 'what is' must be transformed, once and for all, into 'what ought to be', or 'what ought to be' must be accepted as an inevitable condition of 'what is now'. The first alternative, the transformation of 'what is' into 'what ought to be', conveys a certainty and finality. It intimates the project of finding heaven on earth; the Pelagian project of putting one's faith in one's own powers to save oneself. The acceptance of 'what ought to be' as a condition that is discrepant from 'what is' is a far less decisive, certain or neat resolution. In this condition one must accept the limits of one's powers. This response may manifest a stoic *apatheia* to the trials and tribulations of life or give rise to a longing for invariably undeserved grace – the Pauline and Augustinian exercise. When either of the above undertakings gains an unusual degree of intensity and seriousness, on Oakeshott's contention, a self is engaged in a condition that refers beyond the mundane satisfaction of wants and approved conditions; a self becomes concerned with what may appropriately be called its salvation.

In 'Religion and the Moral Life' Oakeshott argued that a religious level of experience addresses who one is rather than who one ought to be: 'What in morality was a mere "should be", in religion becomes an "is".' Part of this address, however, must acknowledge that one *is* always accompanied by a further ought to be. Expressed in terms of the Christian doctrine of original sin, a necessary step in the salvation of a self is the acknowledgment of one's sinful condition. Sin represents the separation of humanity ('what is') from the perfection of God ('what ought to be'). At a religious level of experience the incoherence and incompleteness of life is seen for what it is; it is apprehended without being resolved in this world.[35] In *Experience and Its Modes* Oakeshott continued to reject any suggestion that religion realises, once and for all, what ought to be. On the contrary,

> what is important for religion has always been the profession which is contained in the actual conduct of life. A man who is 'religious' and does not behave in accordance with his 'religious' beliefs may be said to profess one religion and follow another. And there is no doubt which of them should be spoken of as his religion.[36]

The religious life is not to be found in the professions and claims of one's achievements or how others ought to behave. It refers to actual manners of conduct; not beliefs about how the world ought to be, but how it actually is.

Oakeshott's account of religion as completion in 'what is' implies a critique of two common understandings of religious experience. Each of these attitudes separates religion from life and finds in one of these moments only a pale reflection of the other. On the one hand, religion is portrayed as a sweet release from the obstinate interminability of life. The mortal world is rejected for a more permanent truth: 'I live, yet no true life I

---

[35] Cf *Religion, Politics and the Moral Life*, p. 28, 'much of [St Paul's] life was spent in an effort to reconcile the Christian expectation of the end of the world with the disenchanting fact of delay …'

[36] *Experience and Its Modes.*, p. 292.

know' lamented Theresa of Ávila.[37] She understood the illusory character of the mortal world as a divine trial. On the other hand, religion is believed to cover life in illusion; an illusion all the more difficult to overcome for being self-delusion. Religion is rejected as a veil that covers the real character of the world: 'Religion is the sigh of the oppressed creature, the heart of the heartless world and the soul of soulless conditions. It is the *opium* of the people.'[38] Marx understood religious suffering as an ignorant expression of 'real' suffering. Despite explaining the reality of illusion, ultimately both of these positions propose a dichotomy between life and religion in which one moment is deemed an illusory mirage of its other, real counterpart. Theresa strove to overcome the illusory world in the religious realities of the divine and Marx attempted to discover the real world by tearing down the illusory veil of religion.

Characteristically, Oakeshott's account of religious experience as completion in 'what is' steers a middle course between the above positions. Each begins with a half-truth that it mistakes for the whole. With those who hold that a religious level of experience provides truths more permanent than the offerings of a mundane existence, he agreed. Religion does indeed bear out a condition which is more alive than the unreflective presumption of those callous to the mysterious incompleteness in life. However, he rejected any suggestion that religious truths are other-worldly, transcending and thus abandoning the world of mortal experience. To this end he opened his 1929 essay, 'Religion and the World', employing a quotation from Saint James as a foil: 'Pure religion ... is to keep unspotted from the world.' He responded:

---

[37] Theresa of Ávila, *Complete Works* vol. 3, (ed. E.A. Peers) (London, Sheed and Ward, 1975), p. 277.

[38] K. Marx, *A Contribution to the Critique of Hegel's Philosophy of Right* in *Early Writings*, (Penguin, Harmondsworth, 1975), p. 244.

if there be one idea ... that provokes no assent, however qualified, in our minds, it is surely this – that religion consists in
abandoning the world for a cloistered, if virtuous, existence, to
which the word 'life' can scarcely be attributed. Religion, if it
be no more and no other than this, is a pursuit for which we
can find no place in any life we should wish to live, nor any
response from the world of ideals our civilization has made
familiar to us.[39]

With those who denounce religion as mere illusion in life,
then, Oakeshott agreed that religion is *our* experience. He
found this, however, no reason for heaping upon religion a
good many (if not all) of the woes of the world. Those who
would promote life above religion may reject religious dog-
mas as life-destroying or explain them away as a ruling class
conspiracy. But too often they do so by destroying all sense of
the religious mystery at and in life.

Properly understood, then, religious experience is of our
world. It is life and living taken, not to a logical, but to a practical conclusion. Oakeshott argued that religious experience lies
in 'what is' rather than 'what ought to be', although he maintained that neither of these conditions can be asserted without
supposing the other. 'Religion and the Moral Life' and the passage in *Experience and Its Modes* only provide a scant outline of
Oakeshott's account of salvation as completion in 'what is'. He
presented his most concerted account of religion as salvation
in 'what is' in 'Religion and the World' composed between
these works.

In 'Religion and the World' Oakeshott set out two conceptions of salvation in terms of two characters, the 'religious
man' and the 'worldly man'. These characters represent two
systems of value.[40] These systems of value are distinguished
from one another in terms of the relation that each posits

---

[39]   *Religion, Politics and the Moral Life*, p. 27.

[40]   *Ibid.*, p. 31.

between the worth of a self (what ought to be) and that self (what is). A worldly self

> believes in the fundamental stability of the present order, or
> that it will merely evolve into another. The earth we tread, the
> species to which we belong, the history we make ... seem ...
> permanent ... This belief implies what may be described as an
> external standard of value: things are imagined to have some
> sort of worth apart from their value in the life of an individual;
> and consequently, what is prized is success, meaning the
> achievement of some external result.[41]

The worldly worth of a self is measured in achievements
that are external to the self, in the contributions of a self to a
condition perceived to be greater and more permanent than
itself. The self is of value, in fact it might only be said to exist in
any significant sense, in the reflections of its external accomplishments. The permanence and coherence that a self seeks in
living its life 'is sought in external accomplishment, in extent
of knowledge, in a career or in a man's contribution to art or
science.'[42] Salvation lies in a standard outside of the self, a
standard which declares what a self ought to be. In a worldly
system of value, then, salvation is understood in terms of a self
realising or contributing to a condition that is 'what ought to
be which is not now'.

Oakeshott contrasted a worldly system of value with a religious one. A religious system of value inverts the worldly
order of priorities. Instead of a self that finds value in its (external) achievements, a religious system of value holds that the
achievements of a self are only achievements in so far as they
affirm the self. For a religious system of value 'life is too short
and uncertain to be hoarded, too valuable to be spent at the
pleasure of others, of past or of future ... It is simply life itself,
life dominated by the belief ... that if we lose ourselves we lose

---

[41]   *Ibid.*
[42]   *Ibid.*, pp. 32–3.

all.'[43] A self might fail and fail again in establishing a successful career, but these worldly failings provide no indication of
the quality of a self; that is, the religiosity with which a self con-
ducts its life. Herein lies the gist of Oakeshott's observation of
over forty years later that 'Cervantes created a character in
whom the disaster of each encounter with the world was pow-
erless to impugn it as a self-enactment.'[44] A religious system of
value holds the self as its primary object, so that the self is its
own end. Salvation in a religious system of value is understood in terms of a self realising what it is.

Worldly and religious systems of value both refer to the
worth of a self in life. Each system of value rejects, without
denying, the character of the other. These systems of value
contend with one another precisely because they are of the
same world of experience; both assume that change is intrinsic
in the character of experience. If they were different kinds of
experience, they would be logically irrelevant to one another.
Each system of value differs from the other in regards of where
it locates the principles of change and identity. A worldly system of value understands change as issuing from the finitude
of the self (what is) and its inability to realise the principle of
permanency (identity), which is manifest in an external standard (what ought to be). A religious system of value understands change as issuing from the external world and the
principle of permanency as the ability of a self to resist this
transient world by possessing itself.

Worldly and religious systems of value do not describe different parts of the world of conduct; they do not require each
other to constitute a single whole system of value. Rather, a
religious system of value is a complete system in itself, as is its
worldly counterpart. Each system of value offers a different
perspective upon an entire world of experience; each is a lens

---

[43]   *Ibid.*, pp. 34–5.
[44]   *On Human Conduct*, p. 241.

through which life as a whole can be understood. A religious system, for instance, does not describe the 'good' or holy end of a scale of value and a worldly system the 'bad' or evil end of the same scale. A religious system of value is expressed in a self that takes the measure of itself from within itself. It is a system that describes a scale of value which encompasses the most sacred of sacrifices and 'the grandeur of devilry.'[45] The sin of *superbia* committed by Milton's Satan may be the apogee of evil but it has nothing to do with the irreligion of a worldly contempt for his self. Even when cast from Heaven, Satan affirmed his sin, and in his sin, his sinful self, regaling his fallen legions

> What though the field be lost?
> All is not lost; the unconquerable will,
> And study of revenge, immortal hate,
> And courage never to submit or yield:
> And what is else not to be overcome?[46]

Satan measures his worth in terms of a religious system of value. His (inflated) sense of self is the very reason that he embarked upon the course of action that led to his downfall. His fall is a failing only in terms of a worldly system of value; in terms of a religious system of value, his fall is the confirmation of the spiritual mettle that is his quintessential self. A self that realises itself in a religious system of value may have nothing to show but a career of constant or severe failings (like the characters of Don Quixote and Satan), but worldly failure is no indication of religious success. There have also been characters who, although they have enjoyed an extraordinary level of worldly success, have shown a remarkable lack of integrity towards themselves (and Doctor Faustus is perhaps the most sublime image of such a character).

---

[45]   *Ibid.*, p. 84.

[46]   J. Milton, 'Paradise Lost', Bk. 1, Lines 105–09 in *Poetical Works*, (ed. D. Bush) (Oxford, Oxford University Press, 1983), p. 215.

In providing alternative perspectives or lenses through which to view a self, worldly and religious systems of value do not provide a device for sorting the chaff from the wheat of humankind. Every life, indeed, every performance has a worldly and a religious aspect. Even the most religious lives may and often do project significant worldly aspects. Thus the religious ordeal of Francis of Assisi can be ignored for his charitable works, his re-building of the church of Saint Damian and his founding of the Friars Minor. Although Francis's life bears scrutiny in terms of his worldly achievements, this latter category tells us less of the life under consideration (and perhaps more of its contribution to ecclesiastical history).[47] Herein lies Oakeshott's reason for preferring a religious self over a worldly self. A religious system of value gives a more concrete account of the life of a self than a worldly system of value by providing a more certain referent for a self seeking salvation in life. I am not claiming that Oakeshott was in the business of composing edifying discourses recommending that his readers attend to their spiritual health over their worldly affairs.[48] He was, however, arguing that in attending to a religious system of value, a self more surely possesses itself in living its life than in its attendance upon worldly affairs. This theme can be traced through Oakeshott's subsequent works and is re-presented in the most explicit detail in *On Human Conduct*.

---

[47] See G.K. Chesterton, *St Francis of Assisi*, (London, Hodder and Stoughton, 1923). Chesterton showed an awareness of both aspects of Francis's life but devotes a substantially greater proportion of his essay to discussing the religious enactments of Francis rather than his worldly achievements.

[48] Cf. G.W.F. Hegel, *Phenomenology of Spirit* (Trans. A.V. Miller), (Oxford, Oxford University Press, 1977), Sect. 9, p. 5, 'Whoever seeks mere edification, and whoever wants to shroud in mist the manifold variety of this earthly existence and of thought ... may look where he likes to find all this. He will find ample opportunity to dream up something for himself. But philosophy must beware of the wish to be edifying.'

3. Religion and the World as Self-Enactment and Self-Disclosure

On first appearances, Oakeshott's distinction between religious and worldly systems of value equates with his accounts of the morality of the individual and the morality of the anti-individual. Like the religious self, the morality of the individual measures the worth of a self in terms of that self and, like the worldly self, the morality of the anti-individual measures the worth of a self in the approximation of that self to an external measure such as 'the community'. However, the morality of the individual and the morality of the anti-individual are more complex than suggested by this direct equation. Religious and worldly systems of value describe the postulates that underpin the different conceptions of identity implied in the morality of the individual and the morality of the anti-individual.

The essays in which Oakeshott related the historical circumstances of the emergence of the morality of the individual and the morality of the anti-individual contain no explicit reference to the postulates that each disposition implies about the character of conduct. And Oakeshott's most concerted elucidation of the postulates implied in the morality of the individual occurs in the first essay of *On Human Conduct*, 'On the Theoretical Understanding of Human Conduct' in which neither the individual nor the anti-individual are mentioned. He presented no comparable exposition of the postulates implied in the morality of the anti-individual but the distinctive character of the postulates implied in this belief system can be traced in a few references that he made to it in *The Harvard Lectures*. Attending to the postulates that each moral disposition implies about the character of conduct sets a frame of reference in which their respective conceptions of salvation can be observed.

In 'On the Theoretical Understanding of Human Conduct' Oakeshott presented moral conduct as postulating two distinct but inseparable aspects. He called the first of these aspects 'self-disclosure' and the second 'self-enactment'. Self-disclosure is 'the intercourse of agents, each concerned with procuring imagined and wished-for satisfactions (which need not be self-gratifications) and seeking them in the responses of another or other selves.'[49] Because of its substantive and inter-subjective character, the activity of self-disclosure is 'immersed in contingency, it is interminable and it is liable to frustration, disappointment and defeat.'[50] Self-disclosure bears the full force of the ever-changing character of life – agents may be sure of their wants (both for themselves and their world) but they can never be sure of securing the satisfaction of those wants. The wants and satisfactions of other agents nearly always compromise, if not defeat, an intended outcome. Even when a self successfully satisfies its wants in the performances of other agents, a new situation disclosing new wants inevitably usurps this satisfaction.

It should be remembered that practices do not refer to the performances themselves; they qualify performances. Practices in self-disclosure do not specify the particular desires and performances which agents ought to desire and perform in seeking the satisfaction of their wants in the performances of others. Rather, they specify conditions that should be acknowledged in agents choosing their desires and performances. So, Oakeshott's full account of moral conduct as self-disclosure identifies:

> agents disclosing themselves in responding to their contingent situations by choosing what they shall say or what they shall do in relation to imagined and wished-for outcomes, answering one another as seekers and therefore as providers

---

[49]   *On Human Conduct*, p. 70.

[50]   *Ibid.*, p. 73.

of chosen satisfactions, and related to one another in terms of a multiplicity of practices, each composed of considerations to be subscribed to in choosing and doing, and each constituting a specific formal relationship between the participants.[51]

Acknowledging the profound uncertainty inherent in self-disclosure does not preclude conditions that ameliorate its contingent character. A self disclosing itself to other selves, for instance, can be called upon to justify its performances in terms of the moral practices to which these performances ought to subscribe. Thus, a performance such as killing may be justified in terms of the practices of a just war or self-defence, 'notable failure to recognize [appropriate] conditions is to *be guilty.*'[52]

In acknowledging the authority of moral practices, agents may disclose their wants appropriately and judge the propriety of the wants of others. Moral practice mitigates the contingency of self-disclosure:

> in stipulating general conditions for choosing less incidental than the actions themselves, in establishing relationships more durable than those which emerge and melt away in transactions to satisfy a succession of contingent wants, and in articulating rules and duties which are indifferent to the outcome of the actions they govern, it [moral practice] may be said to endow human conduct with a formality in which its contingency is somewhat abated.[53]

In referring to practices in self-disclosure agents mollify the central fact of life, the inevitable mortality of each particular desire and performance. An identity takes shape in spite of its susceptibility to change. But the unsure and ever-changing referents of these moral practices in the wants and perfor-

---

[51] *Ibid.,* p. 59.

[52] *Ibid.,* p. 76, Oakeshott discussed the idiom of justification as an *ex post facto* idiom of persuasion. *Ibid.,* pp. 68–9.

[53] *Ibid.,* p. 74.

mances of the disclosing self and the wants and performances of other selves, constantly undermines and obfuscates the attempts of a self to establish an identity.

The second aspect of moral conduct that Oakeshott identified affords the self a greater degree of shelter from the vicissitudes of life than self-disclosure. He called this aspect self-enactment. Self-enactment is 'conduct in respect of the sentiments or motives in which actions are chosen or performed.'[54] And 'by a motive I mean, not an antecedent drive or tendency or disposition to choose one action … in preference to another, but an agent's sentiment in choosing and performing the actions he chooses and performs … the motive of an action is the action itself considered in terms of the sentiment … in which it is chosen and performed.'[55] Motives are concerned 'not … with recognizing agency in others but with an agent's exercise of his powers in respect of himself.'[56] In self-enactment, then, a self explores its relation with itself rather than another or others.

Self-disclosure is conduct between agents and its inter-subjective character allows other agent's to assess the quality of an agent's disclosures with relative certainty. One can be relatively certain of the character of the disclosures of others – that is, the adequacy of their subscription to commonly acknowledged moral practices in their intercourse with others. The motive in which a self enacts itself is, however, veiled from the scrutiny of others. A just disclosure, for instance, may be performed with a motive that enacts a fearful, a magnanimous or even a malicious self. Hobbes was referring to justice in terms of self-enactment when he declared that the just man acts, not

---

[54] *Ibid.*

[55] *Ibid.*, pp. 71–2.

[56] *Ibid.*, p. 75.

guiltlessly, but from contempt for injustice.[57] And Don Quixote's 'madness' refers to his inappropriate self-disclosures; his enactments are subscriptions to moral practices that constitute a code of chivalric conduct. In self-enactment the self that is enacted is largely mysterious to other agents.

On the above account it might seem that there is no criterion by which the moral character of an agent's self-enactments may be established. Certainly Hobbes took the business of the sovereign to be concerned solely with agents' disclosures, that is, with their guilt or innocence – their enactments are matters for their conscience and God.[58] The lack of an inter-subjective referent does not, however, preclude the possibility of an agent failing to satisfactorily enact himself when 'the enactments and re-enactments of himself … so far forget himself as to affront his own integrity.'[59] The sentiment in which a self chooses to act is not confined merely to one's own opinion of one's conduct but nor do the opinions of others determine the moral character of a self's enactments. It is, rather, the adequacy of a self's motives in subscribing to authoritative practices that determines the moral character of a self enacting

---

[57] Hobbes, *Leviathan*, Ch. 15, Sect. 6, p. 97. 'The names of just, and unjust, when they are attributed to men, signify one thing; and when they are attributed to actions, another. When they are attributed to men they signify conformity, or inconformity of manners, to reason. But when they are attributed to actions, they signify the conformity, of inconformity to reason, not of manners, or manner of life, but of particular actions. A just man therefore, is he that taketh all the care he can, that his actions may be all just: and an unjust man is he who neglecteth it. And such men in our language are more often styled by the names righteous and unrighteous; than just and unjust … the justice of actions denominates men, not just, but *guiltless*: and the injustice of the same, which is also called injury, gives them the name *guilty*.' Cf. *On Human Conduct*, p. 76.

[58] Hobbes, *Leviathan*, Ch. 27, Sect. 2: 'To intend to steal or kill is a sin, though it never appear in word or fact: for God that seeth the thought of man can lay it to his charge: but till it appear by something done, or said, by which the intention may be argued by a human judge it hath not the name of crime …'

[59] *On Human Conduct*, pp. 73–4.

itself. Oakeshott acknowledged that some of his readers may find his inclusion of self-enactment within the bounds of morality unacceptable in removing any inter-subjective criterion of judgement, reward, punishment and so forth. He insisted, however, that this is not a failing in the moral character of self-enactment but is intrinsic to this aspect of moral conduct. He concluded his account of self-enactment by acknowledging that:

> Our moral language may often be confused in its identification of 'virtuous' or 'vicious' sentiments, but it is not undecided whether or not to applaud malice or to disapprobate a motive of good faith or generosity … The compunctions of self-enactment are, then, demands an agent makes upon himself … [and] which cannot be required of him by another … but which are not merely his own good opinion of himself: the requirement of thinking about himself as he should while doing as he ought. Conduct which notably fails to observe this condition is *shameful*.[60]

R.W. Emerson described the rewards and sanctions that refer to self-enactment when he observed that there is a type of justice 'in the soul of man … whose retributions are instant and entire. He who does a good deed is instantly ennobled. He who does a mean deed is by the action itself contracted.'[61] Emerson's account only makes sense when it is realised that he was referring to the aspect of moral conduct that Oakeshott called self-enactment. By contrast, the unjust disclosures of a self, if undetected, can bring substantial (if sometimes short-lived) increase in the capacities and powers of a self.

Self-disclosure and self-enactment describe two distinct but inseparable aspects of conduct within the morality of the individual. On the one hand, self-disclosure refers to the guilt or

---

[60] *Ibid.*, p. 76.

[61] Cited in William James, *The Varieties of Religious Experience: A Study in Human Nature*, (London, Longmans, 1911), p. 32.

innocence of a performance and, on the other, self-enactment refers to the shame or honour of a performance. Guilt is the failure to subscribe adequately to authoritative practices in disclosing wants and seeking the satisfaction of these wants in the performances of others. Shame is the failure to subscribe adequately to authoritative practices in enacting the motives in which performances are chosen. Every performance can be understood either in terms of its innocence or guilt or in terms of its shame or honour. (Even the performances of a hermit in shunning the company of his or her fellows may be understood in terms of self-disclosure, that is, the disclosure of a reclusive self. Furthermore, a hermit may be guilty in not adequately subscribing to authoritative practices, for instance, in committing trespass or avoiding a term of national service.)

Oakeshott described self-disclosure in terms of agents seeking satisfactions in the performances of others and understanding these performances in terms of their innocence or guilt. The practices of self-disclosure refer to a mundane level of conduct where moral achievement is subject to the full force of the transience of life. Oakeshott acknowledged the moral achievement of a self successfully disclosing itself in adventures with other selves. However, he found that these practices refer to an aspect of conduct which is too reliant upon the vicissitudes of life to achieve anything as comprehensive as salvation;

> The inherently episodic character of the diurnal adventures of self-disclosure ... which compose a human life ... is the choice and pursuit of substantive conditions of things [where] every achievement is evanescent, and (as Augustine says) he who thinks otherwise "understands neither what he seeks nor what he is who seeks it".[62]

Twice in the brief exposition of the character of religion in *On Human Conduct* Oakeshott referred to self-disclosure as

[62]   *On Human Conduct*, p. 84.

'the illusion of affairs', language reminiscent of his description of a worldly system of value.[63]

Although Oakeshott did not refer explicitly to self-enactment in terms of seeking salvation, the phrase provides an appropriate frame of reference within which to comprehend agents enacting themselves by understanding their performances in terms of their shame or honour. The association of salvation with self-enactment is confirmed by Oakeshott's inclusion of religious experience within this aspect of moral conduct. On considering the conditions in which a self enacts itself he found the:

> unresolved and inconclusive character of human conduct is qualified (and not merely concealed) ... There is at least the echo of an imperishable achievement when the valour of the agent and not the soon-to-vanish victory ... are the considerations ... [Self-enactment] is never separable from the deadly engagement of agents disclosing themselves in responding to their contingent situations and achieving their passing satisfactions or suffering their transitory disappointments. And the enacted self is itself a fugitive; not a generic unity but a dramatic identity without benefit of a model of self-perfection.'[64]

The dramatic character of an enacted self escapes, as far as is possible, the transience of life by finding eternity in each moment:

> the sharpness of death and the deadliness of doing overcome, and the transitory sweetness of mortal affection, the tumult of grief and the passing beauty of a May morning [are] recognized neither as merely evanescent adventures nor as emblems of better things to come, but as *aventures*, themselves encounters with eternity.[65]

---

[63] *Ibid.*, pp. 84 and 85.

[64] *Ibid.*, p. 84

[65] *Ibid.*, p. 85.

Thus, Oakeshott argued, in self-enactment 'doing is delivered, at least in part, from the deadliness of doing, a deliverance gracefully enjoyed in the quiet of a religious faith.'[66] His description of the fleeting eternity in each moment echoes one of the concluding propositions of Wittgenstein's *Tractatus*: 'If by eternity is understood not endless temporal duration but timelessness, then he lives eternally who lives in the present.'[67]

So, Oakeshott's account of self-enactment and self-disclosure as aspects of moral conduct that provide selves with more or less certain principles of identity evokes his earlier characterisation of worldly and religious systems of value. Self-disclosure and self-enactment identify aspects of moral conduct, just as worldly and religious systems of value are both systems of value. In the way of their predecessors, self-disclosure and self-enactment provide distinct frames of reference in which the worth of a performance (and the self who performs it) may be measured. Just as success in religious enactment reveals nothing of the worldly character of a performance and *vice versa*, so an honourable enactment does not ameliorate the guilt of an unsatisfactory disclosure; a pardon is not an admission of innocence. While Oakeshott refrained from recommending the importance of self-enactment over self-disclosure, he suggested that a self may more surely possess its life by attending to its enactments rather than its disclosures.

If Oakeshott's characterisation of moral conduct as self-enactment and self-disclosure echoes his earlier account of religious and worldly systems of value, a subtle shift in tone should also be acknowledged. A self seeking its worth in terms of a worldly system of value appears to have so poorly understood the principle of identity that it seeks to secure, that it suf-

---

[66]   *Ibid.*, p. 74.

[67]   L. Wittgenstein, *Tractatus Logico-Philosophicus*, (trans. C.K. Ogden) (London, 1922) prop. 6.43 1.1.

fers a moral failing in ever having embarked upon this course of action or understanding of self. By the time Oakeshott had come to characterise self-disclosure as an aspect of moral conduct, however, he could acknowledge success as a moral achievement. Subscription to a worldly system of value or attending to the disclosures of a self provide inadequate security from the change inherent in the world of conduct because the satisfactions they seek refer to the substantive condition of things. Even when self-disclosure is recognised as the subscription to moral rather than prudential practices (a specification absent from his characterisation of a worldly system of value), the fleeting character of the substantive performances and desires that these practices qualify mortally infect the disclosures as a principle of identity.

If Oakeshott's account of self-disclosure more clearly acknowledges it as a moral achievement than is the case with his account of a worldly system of value, his account of the accomplishments in self-enactment are more circumspect than his presentation of the self realised in a religious system of value. The enactments of a self refer to the motives in which substantive performances are undertaken. And while a successful enactment has less to do with the success of the substantive performance in securing sought-after satisfactions than does a disclosure, they are clearly still subject to the inevitable transience that infects the world of conduct. Like the ever-changing formal practices that qualify substantive performances, self-enactment provides a principle of identity that is less transient than the performance to which a motive refers.

4. Salvation in the Morality of the Individual and the Morality of the Anti-Individual

The relation of Oakeshott's account of the appropriate terms in which a self is constituted to other accounts of self within the morality of the individual and the morality of the anti-individual can be mapped in terms of his distinction between self-enactment and self-disclosure. The different relationships postulated between self-enactment and self-disclosure give rise to or underlie different conceptions of salvation. Oakeshott's characterisation of the morality of the individual embraces a broad tradition of thought encompassing liberal thinkers such as Kant, Smith, Bentham, J.S. Mill and Spencer, what might be called ambiguously liberal thinkers such as Hobbes, Burke and Hegel and some of the more strident critics of liberal thought such as Kierkegaard, Dostoevski and Nietzsche.[68] And although the morality of the individual has gained its most forceful expressions in modern times, elements of this tradition are intimated by much earlier thinkers – in, for instance, Aristotle's understanding of *polis*-life in terms friendship rather than as a natural association or as the private dominion of a lord.

Oakeshott argued that thinkers within the tradition of the morality of the individual have tended to recognise moral conduct either as self-disclosure or self-enactment but rarely as both.[69] He noticed, for instance, that

> Some writers (Mill, for example) while not altogether ignoring this feature of human conduct [self-enactment] have denied it any moral significance. To others it has seemed to be not only its most important conditional feature but to be that to which the term 'moral' exclusively refers. Aristotle ... and Kant ... are, perhaps, writers of this persuasion.'[70]

One of the most forthright presentations of moral conduct solely in terms of self-disclosure is Bentham's Greatest Happiness Principle. Because the character of an enactment defies

---

[68] See *On Human Conduct*, p. 71 and *Rationalism in Politics*, p. 376.

[69] Hobbes would meet the criterion as a thinker within the morality of the individual who atributed a moral character to both self-disclosure and self-enactment.

[70] *On Human Conduct*, p. 71

certain scrutiny and assessment, Bentham simply excluded it from his moral calculus. And perhaps one of the most extreme presentations of the over-riding importance of self-enactment is presented in the Kierkegaardian Paradox.[71] Kierkegaard argued that Abraham had a duty of faith to God to slay his son regardless of the grotesque disclosure entailed in such a performance. It is important to note, however, that even in the most extreme cases of Bentham and Kierkegaard, there is no collapse of either aspect into the other. Bentham did not deny self- enactment but only its relevance in calculating the Greatest Happiness and thus its moral character. And Kierkegaard did not deny self-disclosure as a distinct aspect of conduct. He was, in fact, arguing that satisfactory self-disclosure should not be mistaken for an adequate moral life.

Oakeshott's distinction between self-disclosure and self-enactment places his work squarely within the tradition of the morality of the individual. However, he argued that, properly understood, self-disclosure and self-enactment are both aspects of moral conduct. Without a moral sanction supporting self-disclosures, society would fall into a state of anarchy where the moral integrity of each agent could not save the commonwealth; in fact, in times of crisis, enthusiasm for virtue and righteousness may contribute to its disintegration.[72] However, establishing the moral character of self-disclosure

[71] S.A. Kierkegaard, *Fear and Trembling*, 'Speech in Praise of Abraham', (trans. A. Hannay) (Harmondsworth, Penguin, 1985), pp. 49–56.

[72] Cf. *On Human Conduct*, p. 78, 'The members of the Order which constituted the Abbaye de Thélème dispensed with rules and duties to govern their conduct and took as their Rule a precept about how they should think when acting: the Augustinian principle of conduct, "Love and do what you will." But, Rabelais tells us, this was a sufficient Rule, not because "virtuous" sentiment suffices, nor because the Thélèmites had been miraculously redeemed from inclination to incontinent self-assertion in their adventures in self-disclosure, but because they were well-born, well-bred and well-educated in a language of moral intercourse.'

does not provide the grounds for Oakeshott excluding self-enactment from his account of moral conduct. When it does not acknowledge the moral character of self-enactment, the morality of the individual suffers from precisely the sort of spiritual bankruptcy attributed to it by some of the most vehement critics of liberal thought. These critics issue both from within the tradition of the morality of the individual (for example, Kierkegaard, Dostoevski and Nietzsche who distinguished enactments from disclosures and the moral character of the former over the latter) and from within the tradition of the morality of the anti-individual (for example, Rousseau, Marx, and Wagner who did not distinguish between enactments and disclosures).

Oakeshott's account of the character of morality presupposed in the morality of the anti-individual is far more cursory than the morality of the individual. In *The Harvard Lectures* he stated that the 'distinction between crime and sin is one of the characteristics of modern European societies.'[73] He qualified this claim, acknowledging that the distinction has been made in societies beyond modern Europe and, more significantly, that not all societies in modern Europe have acknowledged this distinction. (In this respect some modern European societies have been less 'modern' than others.) The denial of the distinction between crime and sin is a postulate about the character of conduct made within the tradition of the morality of the anti-individual. The morality of the anti-individual recognises 'every crime … as a sin and every sin is proscribed as a crime …'[74] To commit theft is, for instance, not merely to be guilty of criminal activity in stealing from 'the people' (the morality of the anti-individual acknowledges no mine and thine), it is also a sinful act. No motive could provide a reason

---

[73]   M. Oakeshott, *Morality and Politics in Modern Europe: The Harvard Lectures* (ed. S.R. Letwin), (New Haven, Yale University press, 1993), pp. 16-7.

[74]   *The Harvard Lectures*, p.16.

for committing a crime and so introduce the possibility of pardon. To plead to be excused for a crime on the grounds that an illegal act was performed in a motive of compassion merely exacerbates the moral failing in revealing a lack of appreciation of the moral enormity committed. Crime by definition is iniquitous. The obverse is also the case. To behave guiltlessly but without enthusiasm for justice is sinful and sin belies crime.[75]

The identification of crime with sin postulated in the morality of the anti-individual appears as a cardinal feature distinguishing it from the morality of the individual. Oakeshott identified accounts of conduct within the morality of the individual that deny the moral character of either self-disclosure or self-enactment. Accounts that identify moral conduct solely in terms of self-disclosure (as in Oakeshott's reading of Mill) exclude self-enactment from *moral* conduct, but they do not deny the distinctive character of this aspect of conduct. And accounts that identify moral conduct solely in terms of self-enactment (as in Oakeshott's reading of Kant and Aristotle) exclude self-disclosure from *moral* conduct, but they do not deny the distinctive character of this aspect of conduct. Both cases draw a distinction between self-disclosure and self-enactment (although Oakeshott disagreed that the distinction is between moral and non-moral types of conduct).

It is precisely the distinction between self-disclosure and self-enactment that is denied in the morality of the anti-individual. The morality of the anti-individual allows no distinction between crime and sin or, in other words, law and conscience: all crime is sin and obversely a performance from a corrupt motive is, regardless of its apparent guiltlessness, a crime. In fact, apparent innocence may further compound the

---

[75]   M. Oakeshott, *The Politics of Faith and the Politics of Scepticism* (ed. T. Fuller), (New Haven, Yale University Press, 1996), p. 97, refers to 'The Greek muleteer who when asked why he beat his animal, which was going very well, replied, "Yes, but he doesn't want to go ..."'

'sin of crime' by adding to the initial transgression evidence of an accomplishment in the art of deceit or a lack of remorse. The morality of the anti-individual conflates sin and crime so that these aspects of conduct are indistinguishable as well as inseparable one from the other. There is no distinction between practices that refer to the guilt or innocence of the performances of agents interacting with one another and practices that refer to the shame or honour of the motives in which performances are enacted. This conflation of sin and crime imparts an impossible character to conduct. The result of laying bare the interior life of an agent to external criteria treats the agent as an automaton.

In *Experience and Its Modes* Oakeshott defined religious experience as arising whenever a life is lived at a high scale of intensity and seriousness. On this definition both the morality of the individual and the morality of the anti-individual will have religious analogues, both moral characters have instances in which they have been possessed of an intensity that could appropriately be described as religious. In elucidating the character of religious intensity that is intimated within the morality of the individual in a self attending to its enactments, Oakeshott stated 'What is sought in religious belief is not merely consolation for woe or deliverance from the burden of sin, but a reconciliation to nothingness.'[76] This statement does not support any particular creed or cosmological view. The nothingness to which one is reconciled is not a claim that there is nothing beyond life in this world; it is a reconciliation to the impermanence in life in our present mortal condition. The reconciliation takes the form of 'making the difficult exchange of hope for faith.'[77] And, once again, faith refers here not to an object of faith beyond life but to the condition of faith in life, that is the state of having faith in the significance of

[76]   *On Human Conduct*, pp. 83–4.
[77]   *Ibid.*, p. 65.

one's present condition instead of a mere hope that a condition of greater significance or permanence can be attained. Oakeshott's final word on religious experience sheds further light on what I believe he was getting at. In his last correspondence with Patrick Riley, he announced:

> during the last couple of years since I came to live here [in Dorset], spending much of my time re-reading all the books which I first read 50 or 60 years ago, I have gone back to theology – or rather, reflection upon religion. And I would like, more than anything else, to extend those brief pages in *On Human Conduct* into an essay … on religion, and particularly on Christian religion … What I would like to write is a new version, a post-Montaigne version of Anselm's *Cur deus homo* in which (amongst much else) 'salvation', 'being saved', is recognized as [having] nothing whatever to do with the *future*.[78]

It is my contention that there are enough references to religious experience in Oakeshott's work to establish more than a glimpse of what his post-Montaigne version of *Cur deus homo* would look like.

In addition to the ground already travelled, further significance can be found in Oakeshott's reference to Anselm's work. The subject of which Anselm's book treated is why God became man. This subject reaffirms the orthodox Christian view that the incarnation is necessary to the salvation of humanity. Humanity is of its own power imperfectable. Imperfectability does not refer to an imperfect condition that can be made perfect – it is a condition, not a problem to be solved. The morality of the individual intimates a conception of salvation in which life and the self are accepted for what they are. The self may possess itself in a dignified withdrawal from the illusion of worldly affairs or by fervently lobbying

---

[78] Letter from Oakeshott to Riley, 1988, cited in P. Riley, 'Michael Oakeshott, Political Philosopher', The Cambridge Review, (October, 1991), p. 113.

the undeserved grace of God.[79] Both of these responses recognise the limits that the character of life imposes on a self and that these limits are not able to be transcended by a self in conduct.

Oakeshott never set out an account of the character of salvation that arises in the conflation of sin and crime postulated in the morality of the anti-individual. However, using what has been discerned of the order of salvation intimated in the morality of the individual we may begin to trace an outline of its character. The morality of the anti-individual rejects the distinction between sin and crime, there is no distinction between religion and the world. The morality of the anti-individual has a strong sense of the imperfections that accompany the present condition in life. However, the conflation of sin and crime supposes an ability to judge not only the moral quality of the actions of a self but the very interior character of the self. Every present source of imperfection must be capable of detection and eradication and thus salvation lies not in the present but in some future condition. A defining characteristic of this future condition is that it is understood to be of this world. Perfection will be realised as the result of the exercise of human powers, the removal of the damned from a rule of saints. The morality of the anti-individual has both theistic and atheistic versions. The theistic versions have looked to establish the conditions in which the unregenerate are purged to make way for a Second Coming. And atheistic versions have been intent on showing how a belief in perfection beyond life is merely a dupe to maintain current imperfections. Any conception of salvation in the morality of the anti-individual refers to a condition that is not now but will be in the future.

---

[79]   See Chesterton, *Orthodoxy*, pp. 223–4. 'The Buddhist saint always has his eyes shut, while the Christian saint always has them very wide open. The Buddhist saint has a sleek harmonious body, but his eyes are heavy with sleep. The mediaeval saint's body is wasted to its crazy bones, but his eyes are frightfully alive.'

Present enjoyments are viewed as at worst distractions from, and at best resources to be sacrificed or used in, the pursuit of future perfection.

One further characteristic of the idea of salvation implied in the conflation of sin and crime that underpins the morality of the anti-individual is the removal of the distinction between moral practices that qualify substantive performances (self-disclosure) and moral practices that refer to the integrity of motives (self-enactment). The removal of this distinction reduces the terms of moral conduct to practices that at best qualify the pursuit of a substantive order of things and at worst actually refer to a substantive condition. Rather than the moral quality of a self being understood in terms of motives that have a formal referent, a cowardly or courageous act for instance, a self is understood in the achievement or promotion of a substantive condition. And achievement in terms of substantive conditions, desires and performances is subject to the full force of the transience of life. The disastrous consequence for the morality of the individual in reducing conduct to substantive performances is particularly apparent in Oakeshott's characterisation of the appropriate terms of moral association.

Chapter 4
Authority and Desire in Moral Association

Oakeshott provided his most extensive characterisations of the morality of the individual and the morality of the anti-individual in terms of their respective understandings of the proper office of government; by which he meant 'what should governments do'. Questions of what government should do introduce considerations of a political nature. And the entry of politics upon the scene invites consideration not only of what governments should do, but the terms in which association, particularly the state, is appropriately constituted. So, the following chapter explores Oakeshott's account of the individual and the anti-individual in terms of their responses to Lewis's first class of moral consideration, the appropriate conditions for establishing harmony and fair play between individuals. Exploring Oakeshott's account of the terms in which the individual and the anti-individual conceive of the appropriate principles of association provides another dimension to his account of each of these characters. The following chapter differs from considerations of Oakeshott's characterisation of modes of association, what has passed for his 'political philos-

ophy', in that it treats the modes of association not as significant in themselves, but for the light they shed on the
individual and the anti-individual. As was the case on exploring Oakeshott's writings on religious experience, the essays in
which he characterised the appropriate terms of association do
not refer to the individual or the anti-individual. Once again,
however, these figures can be found standing behind much of
what he wrote.

1. Authority and Desirability as Principles of Association

In two pieces both dated 1925 Oakeshott inquired after the
character of moral association as realised in the state; the
unpublished *Some Matters Preliminary to a Discussion of Political
Philosophy* and a posthumously published essay, entitled
'Some Remarks on the Nature and Meaning of Sociality'.[1]
These works posit an idea of morality as a distinctively human
quality. In 'The Meaning of Sociality' Oakeshott distinguished
between natural society, which arises in gregarious instincts,
impulses and needs, and human society, which is constituted
in terms of moral relations and the satisfaction of wants.
Accordingly, the moral condition of sociality is distinguished
from mere sociability, which refers to one's physical proximity
to others of one's species.[2] To make his point Oakeshott argued
that sociality is often most comprehensively realised in a life of
solitude when 'The recluse ... does not draw apart in order to
break his connections with the world but in order to find them,
and make them stronger and more vital.'[3] The sociality of the
recluse dispels 'the notion that society may be properly

---

[1]   Published in *Religion Politics and the Moral life*, pp. 46–62.

[2]   *Ibid.*, pp. 49–52.

[3]   *Ibid.*, p. 54.

defined as the opposite to solitude ...'[4] In this essay he asserted that 'we can have no clear view of the nature of society until we have penetrated the secrets of the self.'[5] This is not a claim for the priority of self over society, but rather a statement of how Oakeshott intended to proceed in his inquiry. He maintained throughout this essay that 'A society may be looked at from two sides, we may see it made up of individual selves, and we may see it as making, as being the substance of, those selves. The one is not more an abstraction than the other ...'[6] The constitutive principle, of which self and society are one-sided abstractions, is sociality.

Oakeshott also presented an account of self and society as distinctive sides of sociality in the fourth, fifth and sixth chapters of *Some Matters Preliminary*, entitled respectively, 'The State', 'The Self' and 'The State and the Self'. As in the case of his early metaphysical endeavours and his writings on religion, the influences of Idealist thinkers like Hegel and Bradley are evident in his account of the state. For these thinkers 'the State' denoted an order of experience much more comprehensive than the arrangements of government.[7] The state is not an external constraint upon an individual as is provided, for instance, in Herbert Spencer's *The Man Versus The State*; the state is constitutive of the individual. In *Some Matters Preliminary*, Oakeshott defined the State as consisting:

---

[4]   *Ibid.*

[5]   *Ibid.*, p. 52.

[6]   *Ibid.*, p. 46.

[7]   See *Some Matters Preliminary*, p. 55, Oakeshott cited L. P. Jacks, *Shams and Realities*, (1923), p. 55, 'If politics meant in modern practice what they meant for Plato, Aristotle or Dante, then it would be impossible to exaggerate their importance. But unfortunately they have come to mean something else.' The ancient Hellenic conception of *polis*-life is a far more comprehensive idea than the modern European conception of politics and approaches much more closely what Oakeshott meant by the State in his early works than any modern idea of politics or government.

of a vast number of social, that is moral influences; these come upon us in our intercourse with the members of our society, and in so far as we become true members of that association we are communing with its mind whenever we contemplate its laws, institutions, art, literature, tastes and prejudices. This is the sum of our social experience as it is presented to us in our state.[8]

Two points are of interest in this passage. First, Oakeshott identified the State as the sum of all social relations and, second, he described these social relations as moral influences. All social relations, familial, legal, and any number of pursuits for which individuals join together, religious, cultural, economic or simply for the sake of amusement, are included within the sphere of 'the State'. So, each of these relations constitutes, in some degree, a moral relation.

Oakeshott's first published consideration of the character of the state is an essay published in 1929 and entitled 'The Authority of the State'. He maintained the view, enunciated in *Some Matters Preliminary,* that the state describes one's social (that is moral) relations in their entirety. So, 'Government and law, economic, religious, intellectual and every other activity and aspect of social life find their explanation in this totality; it is to perfect this, and not merely themselves, that they exist.' [9] However, he added to the position stated in *Some Matters Preliminary* by specifying the relation of the state to each of these social relations, arguing that each is related to the state, not as a part to a whole but, as an abstraction of the whole.

Oakeshott distinguished the specifically moral character of the state from other (morally) superficial details in terms of the authority of the state. For Oakeshott, as for Hobbes before him, the hallmarks of authority are indivisibility and irresponsibil-

---

[8]   *Religion, Politics and the Moral Life,* p. 70.
[9]   *Ibid.,* p. 83.

ity and, in the style of the British Idealists, he added completeness.[10] That which has authority answers to no other, thus

> A policeman is not himself authoritative, but draws his
> authority from the law; while the law, as such, is not itself
> authoritative because, if it has feet of its own, still requires
> some ground upon which to stand them. That alone is authori-
> tative which ... stands upon itself.[11]

Oakeshott acknowledged his debt to Hobbes's account of indivisible and irresponsible authority (what Hobbes called sovereignty) by concluding his essay with the epigram that adorns
the frontispiece of the *Leviathan*: '*Non est potestas super terram
quae comparetur ei*' [No authority on earth can be compared to
him].[12] However, whereas Hobbes argued for the authority of
the sovereign understood as the executive and legislative
power, in 'The Authority of the State' Oakeshott considered
legal authority to be predicated authority and thus an abstraction of authority. He agreed with Hobbes on the irresponsible
and indivisible character of authority and that authority is the
exclusive possession of the state, however, he diverged from
Hobbes's position in conceiving of the state in far broader
terms than sovereignty. For Oakeshott, the state refers in its
most comprehensive terms to a way of life.

In Oakeshott's subsequent writings the authoritative character of 'the state' of the 1920s is specified as 'the social whole'
in the '30s, 'civil society' in the '40s and '50s, 'civil association'

---

[10] *Ibid.*, pp. 78–9.

[11] 'Authority of the State: Reply of Mr. Oakeshott [to G.E.G. Caitlin]' in
      Religion, Politics and the Moral Life, p. 89.

[12] *Religion, Politics and the Moral Life*, p 87. Fuller translates *potestas* as
      'power' but, in keeping with Oakeshott's reading of Hobbes, a distinc-
      tion ought to be maintained between the natural 'obligation' of a physi-
      cal power (*potentia*) and moral right in authority (*potestas*).

in the '60s and 70s and finally as 'the rule of law' in the '80s.[13] The changing terminology is not merely cosmetic. These terms all refer to the authoritative character of moral practices. However, each term differs from its predecessor in reflecting a more specific account of the origin of authority (which is nothing other than authority itself). 'The State' and 'the social whole' describe every social relation as the manifestation of a moral practice. 'Civil society' distinguishes civil practices which refer to morality from prudential practices which refer to the satisfaction of desires, implying that not all social relations are moral practices.[14] Herein lies the beginning of Oakeshott's distinction between moral practices and prudential or instrumental practices. 'Civil association' is an even more specific term again, indicating that Oakeshott was considering a peculiarly modern conception of authority. An association, rather than 'a society' or 'a community', implies relations between individuals and, thus, a 'morality of the individual'.[15] And 'the rule of law' is a restatement of the character of civil association. Oakeshott presented his most rigorous account of the character of authority as the idea of civil

---

[13] Oakeshott refers to 'the State' in *Some Matters Preliminary* and 'The Authority of the State' in the 1920s, 'the social whole' in 'The Claims of Politics' in 1939, 'civil society' in his introduction to *Leviathan* in 1946, 'civil society' is changed to 'civil association' in his essays on Hobbes re-published in *Hobbes on Civil Association* and the idea of 'civil association' is also developed in 'On the Civil Condition' both published in the 1970s and he refers to 'the rule of law' in 'The Rule of Law' published in *On History and Other Essays,* (Oxford, Basil Blackwell, 1983).

[14] This distinction is particularly important in understanding Oakeshott's reading of Hobbes. See 'The Moral Life in the Writings of Thomas Hobbes' in *Rationalism in Politics*, pp. 295–350.

[15] See *Rationalism in Politics*, p. 369, the 'rights appropriate to individuality, were not privileges of a single class; they were the property of every subject alike. Each signified the abrogation of some feudal privilege ... What had been a 'community' came to be recognized as an 'association' of individuals ...'

association in the second essay in *On Human Conduct*, 'On the Civil Condition'.

Oakeshott's conception of civil association, like that of 'the State', comprehends social relations as moral practices but, unlike 'the State', it makes a categorial distinction between social relations that are relations of authority, and social relations that are not authoritative. In Weberian fashion Oakeshott called civil association an ideal mode of association that is categorially distinct from other modes of association. In calling civil association an 'ideal' mode of association Oakeshott was not referring to 'ideal' in the everyday sense of being the most desirable state of affairs.[16] Civil association is ideal in so far as its characteristics are logically necessary. An ideal character is a system of characteristics 'detached from its contingent circumstances and ... combined to compose [its] features.'[17] The identity 'civil association' arises out of historically contingent and ambiguous circumstances but these circumstances are of no account when considering it as an ideal character.

Civil association excludes, without denying, the blood ties of kinship and bonds of friendship as well as relations that come about between individuals involved in common and transactional enterprises. Other modes of association may specify other types of practices, but they cannot stand in the place of civil association because they are not relations of authority. The relation between friends is not an authoritative relation and the predicated notion of parental 'authority' has

---

[16] Cf. Franco, *The Political Philosophy of Michael Oakeshott*, p. 179. Civil association is not 'some sort utopia ... it is an identity that has been purged of the contingencies and ambiguities of historic conditions.' Yet this observation does not prevent Franco from writing occasionally as if the historical identity *societas* is equivalent with the ideal identity civil association and the historical identity *universitas* is equivalent with the ideal identity enterprise association.

[17] *On Human Conduct*, p. 4.

more to do with being a parent than it has with authority. As for subscription to a practice out of prudential considerations, Oakeshott did not regard this as a moral practice at all! Oakeshott described civil association as 'a practice ... which is unlike some other practices in being composed entirely of rules; the language of civil intercourse is a language of rules; [civil association] is rule-articulated association.'[18] In presenting civil association as consisting entirely of rules, he argued that the authority of civil rules derives from these rules themselves. Authority is thus irresponsible; it is a self-limiting because self-authenticating practice. In other words, civil rules do not derive their authority from any origin or end outside of association, for instance, from their utility in promoting a desired condition. And individuals do not bear authority because of who they are but because of the offices they hold, offices that are constituted in terms of rules.

Oakeshott contended that the authority of a civil rule is independent of the choice or approval of an individual under its jurisdiction. Civil association is compulsory association:

> the attribution of authority to a rule is not a matter of choice but of subjecting what purports to be authoritative to a certain test and giving reasons for a conclusion; and [civil association] itself provides [these] reasons which, because it is composed of rules, must themselves be rules.'[19]

Thus a civil rule is shown to be authoritative by establishing its authenticity. Authentic civil rules:

> may be good, bad or indifferent (although they cannot have these qualities in instrumental relation to a common purpose),

---

[18]   *Ibid.*, p. 124. Oakeshott describes the relation of a moral rule to a moral practice in *Ibid.*, pp. 66–7 'Moral rules are abridgments [of moral practices] ... What a moral practice intimates as, in general, proper to be said or done, a moral rule makes more explicit in declaring what it is *right* to do ... Rules, duties, and their like moral principles and dogma are ... passages of stringency in a moral practice.'

[19]   *Ibid.*, p. 151.

they may be more or less effective in evoking conduct which adequately subscribes to them, they may be old or recent, they may or may not have been expressly enacted … but their property as rules … is in respect of their being known (or ascertainable) and in respect of their authority.[20]

Oakeshott argued that an agent might escape the jurisdiction of an authoritative rule either by showing why it does not apply to this or that chosen action in this or that particular circumstance or by invoking another authoritative rule that is more pertinent in the circumstances. Inquiries about the authority of this or that rule do not challenge the authoritative character of the rule but request an authoritative specification be made of the rule's jurisdiction in a specific instance. In civil association agents may not choose the conditions of justice but only whether they will behave justly or unjustly.[21]

So, civil rules cannot require agents to choose a particular substantive performance. They merely set out the formal conditions that the substantive performances of agents acknowledge with varying degrees of adequacy. If an agent chooses a substantive performance which does not adequately subscribe to the formal condition prescribed by an authoritative rule, that agent is not by his or her action dissociated from the association, rather he or she is liable to be punished. Oakeshott's account of authority as springing from civil rules whose jurisdiction is beyond the choice of an individual flies in the face of a great deal of contemporary political theory. A

---

[20]   *Ibid.*, pp. 154–5.

[21]   J. Liddington, 'Oakeshott: Freedom in a Modern European State'in *Concepts of Liberty in Political Theory*, (ed. J.N. Gray and Z. Pelczynski), (London, Athlone Press, 1984), pp. 289–320 focuses upon Oakeshott's account of the distinctive types of freedom enjoyed in civil and enterprise modes of association.

more familiar view of authority understands it on the analogy of a contractual relation, and contracts are voluntary.[22]

Contractual accounts of authority understand obligation as deriving from the consent of an individual to be obligated. Without an individual's (express or tacit) consent a rule has no authority. Oakeshott objected that contractual accounts of authority confuse the choice to subscribe adequately or inadequately to authoritative rules in one's performances with the choice of whether these rules are authoritative or not. He argued that an individual

> may make a promise and thus put himself within the jurisdiction and under the authority of the rule that promises should be honoured. But although he does this in a chosen transaction … and although he can fulfil obligations only in a chosen action which subscribes to its conditions, he does not choose the terms of the obligation …[23]

Oakeshott agreed with contractual accounts of authority that individuals have a choice in how they will subscribe to a moral practice, that is whether or not they will choose performances that will adequately subscribe to the practice. He disagreed with contractual accounts, however, if they imply that the authority of a rule, that is, the terms of its obligation, relies upon the consent of an individual to be obligated; an agent has no choice in what is and what is not authoritative.

---

[22]   Franco alludes to problems associated with contractarian theories of the state when he notices that 'In vain do we search [Rawls's] *A Theory of Justice* for a sustained discussion of [authority which is an] absolutely crucial concept (though we do find a rather lengthy defense of civil disobedience).' See *The Political Philosophy of Michael Oakeshott*, pp. 234-5. R.E. Flathman presents a case for the benefits which civil disobedience brings to the practice of authority in *The Practice of Political Authority: Authority and the Authoritative*, (Chicago, University of Chicago Press, 1980), Ch. 6, 'Authority, the Merits of Rules, and Civil Disobedience', yet he maintains the primacy of the practice of authority.

[23]   *On Human Conduct*, p. 156.

Oakeshott brought his definition of civil association into relief by juxtaposing it with a categorially distinct mode of association that he called enterprise association. In enterprise association the validity of rules issues not from the terms of association – not from the rules themselves – but from their promotion of the enterprise or purpose for which the association has been established. Rules in enterprise association do not constitute the association, they are incidental to it.[24] Rules gain their legitimacy from the voluntary choice of associates to be associated in an enterprise and thus it could be appropriate to understand enterprise association on the analogy of contract. On Oakeshott's account of enterprise association, agency manifests itself in the choice of agents to become associated or not to associate, their choice to remain associated or to dissociate themselves from the enterprise that is afoot.

The purpose for which enterprise associates join together need not be a common purpose or a collective good; it may consist of agents seeking their own satisfactions in the responses of others. Thus, subscription to enterprise rules may issue from a prudential considerations of self-interest. This latter type of enterprise association may be seen in a market place, where there is a notable absence of any common purpose or common interest. Because of the voluntary character of enterprise association, enterprise rules may demand substantive performances from associates without infringing their integrity as moral agents. In the event of enterprise associates feeling compromised in what they have been requested or are required to do, they have the choice to dissociate. The freedom of an agent in enterprise association lies, then, not in the choice between substantive performances which subscribe (or do not

---

[24]   Thus enterprisers may remain associated in terms of an enterprise even when they have rejected the validity of certain enterprise rules. See *Ibid.*, p. 117.

subscribe) to a formal authoritative rule, but in the choice to be associated.[25]

'On the Civil Condition' focuses primarily upon the character of civil association, that is, the practice of authority. Oakeshott's account of the character of enterprise association occurs as a foil, setting out conditions that are commonly mistaken for the practice of authority. However, he wrote enough about the character of enterprise association to suggest that if the *authority* of rules is the appropriate consideration in civil association, then the *desirability* of rules is the appropriate consideration in enterprise association. Thus, in 'The Rule of Law', he argued that in enterprise association 'the validity of a recommendation contained in a maxim or precept and its desirability or worth as a piece of advice are indistinguishable; both lie in its sagacity or utility – that is, in the outcome of following it being (or being likely to be) the substantive satisfaction sought.'[26] The prudential character of enterprise association is appropriately expressed in terms of the desirability of its rules.

The desirability of rules in enterprise association does not preclude agents forming enterprise associations *for* moral purposes. Examples of enterprise associations with moral purposes may be found in charitable, religious and political organisations. In these associations, however, the purpose and not the association is moral and thus the seat of 'authority'; the association *qua* association is only incidentally or conditionally authoritative. Enterprise association is authoritative only in so far as it promotes conditions that are desirable in terms of the enterprise and thus the prudential language of enterprise association is, at best, a quasi-moral language.

---

[25] Oakeshott's most detailed account of the type of freedom encountered in enterprise association is set out in 'The Political Economy of Freedom' in *Rationalism in Politics*.

[26] *On History*, pp. 128–9.

Oakeshott's focus upon civil association has been mistaken by some critics of *On Human Conduct* as indicating a hostility towards enterprise association.[27] Responding to a symposium on *On Human Conduct* in which many of the participants mistook his concern with civil association as a rejection of the validity of enterprise association as a mode of association, he retorted that 'the only "animosity" I have ever entertained towards "community" or association in terms of a substantive purpose [that is, enterprise association] is concerned with the attribution of this character to a state or the attempt to impose it upon a state.'[28] While Oakeshott accepted that states involve themselves in a much wider range of activity than the practice of authority, he remained adamant that it is their character as authoritative associations, and not some other quality, which makes them recognisable as states and authoritative associations are compulsory associations.

If states are understood as enterprise associations, agency is compromised in either one of two ways. Either, enterprise association is deemed to be compulsory so that not only must agents acknowledge the authority of conditions prescribed by the state, but they must find these conditions desirable. Such a requirement describes a condition that 'sever[s] the link between belief and conduct which constitutes moral agency'.[29] This situation is inimical to a morality of the individual. Or, the authority of a state is deemed to rest upon the desirability of the conditions that it prescribes. This circumstance reduces authority to desirability and the desirability of conditions is contingent upon an agent's consent. Oakeshott followed Hobbes in arguing that in this circumstance compulsory asso-

---

[27]   For example, see H.F. Pitkin, 'Inhuman Conduct and Unpolitical Theory: Michael Oakeshott's *On Human Conduct*', *Political Theory*, 4 (1976), p. 310.

[28]   'On Misunderstanding Human Conduct', p. 367.

[29]   *On Human Conduct*, p. 158.

ciation can only be maintained through the exercise of coercive power: *potentia* in the absence of *potestas*.[30] Oakeshott's categorial distinction between civil and enterprise association sunders considerations of authority from considerations of desirability, arguing that as principles of association – considerations of the one type cannot be mistaken for considerations of the other without denying the conditions of agency. If the characteristics of these modes of association are confused with one another, if agents are compelled to acknowledge authoritative conditions in terms of their desirability or if authority is reduced to considerations of desirability, then the morality of the individual is destroyed. A morality of the anti-individual has prevailed.

The compromise of moral agency that arises when desirability is taken as the primary characteristic of authoritative rules or when an authority is imposed upon rules that are appropriately subscribed to on the prudential grounds of their desirability recollects Nettleship's identification of the two extremes at which identity breaks down. If authoritative rules are mistakenly understood as requiring acknowledgement only because of their desirability, the association dissipates. Only the imposition of a power approaching a force of nature, that treats individuals as less than agents, can maintain association in this circumstance. In the event of an authority being attributed to rules that are appropriately considered in terms of their desirability, stagnation has supervened upon the association. Agents can no longer exercise the agency postulated by enterprise association and dissociate.

---

[30] Although Hobbes famously argued that covenants without the sword are but words (*Leviathan*, Ch. 14, Sect. 15, p. 89), he also exhibited an awareness that regimes could not rest (let alone be built) upon bayonets alone. Oakeshott explores 'the chicken or the egg' problem that arises in Hobbes's account of commonwealth by institution in *Rationalism in Politics*, pp. 344–50. Briefly, the problem appears in the form that covenants in the state of nature have no certainty because there is no public sword, but a public sword comes about through an original covenant.

Understanding the confusion of civil and enterprise modes of association as giving rise to Nettleship's two extremes at which individuality breaks down also recalls the primary characters of these modes. Civil association consists of authoritative rules that, of themselves, refer only incidentally to substantive performances and desired substantive conditions. Civil association is constituted purely in terms of formal rules, there is no suggestion of an end or purpose in subscribing to civil rules. Enterprise association consists of prudential rules that may provide adverbial conditions that possess a utility in choosing substantive performances, but which also refer to substantive performances and desired substantive conditions. Enterprise association is constituted in terms of a desired substantive condition that is an ought to be but not now. Thus as a principle of identity, enterprise association conveys all the uncertainty of a self attending to the desired substantive conditions of things. The removal of any distinction between the characters of formal moral practices and substantive performances reduces all relations in an association to desirability understood in terms of the promotion of a designated enterprise. This situation describes a condition that is as hostile to individuality as the conflation of sin and crime.

2. Authority and Desirability in Civil Association

Oakeshott's categorial distinction between civil and enterprise modes of association and his account of the catastrophic consequences for agency in confusing this distinction appears to confine considerations of the principles of association in terms of their authority and desirability exclusively within their respective civil and enterprise modes. His account is, however, once again far more complex than this. I have already alluded to the possibility of enterprise association acquiring a quasi-moral character when particular enterprises are understood in moral terms as in the case of charitable, religious or political organisations. In these instances, however, whether it is acknowledged or not, the morality of the enterprise is only a secondary aspect of association in its capacity as association – the primary quality of enterprise *association* remains the desirability of the conditions which it prescribes in relation to the enterprise. Oakeshott devoted little time to discussing the relationship of 'authority' to desirability in enterprise association because in this mode of association all terms of association are understood as expressions of desirability. However, he considered the relation between considerations of rules in terms of their authority and considerations of rules in terms of their desirability within civil association (which he called 'politics') in considerable detail on a number of occasions.[31]

Oakeshott's first published consideration of the character of political activity is a short essay entitled 'The Claims of Politics'. And from a future professor of political science, writing on the eve of the Second World War, his readers might expect a defence of parliamentary democracy and perhaps a lament at the failure of a healthy political culture to have become more securely established in the more recently founded states of Europe. His audience is, however, given nothing of the sort. Instead, Oakeshott turned upon political activity itself, vilifying it as entailing:

> A limitation of view, which appears so clear and practical, but which amounts to little more than a mental fog ... A mind fixed and callous to all subtle distinctions, emotional and intellectual habits become bogus from repetition and lack of examination, unreal loyalties, delusive aims, false significances are what political action involves. And this is so, not because the politically active are under the necessity of persuading the mentally obtuse before their activity can succeed;

---

[31] See 'On the Civil Condition', Sect. 9 and 'The Vocabulary of a Modern European State', *Political Studies*, 23 (1975), Pt. 2 and 'The Rule of Law', Sect. 7.

the spiritual callousness involved in political action belongs to its character, and follows from the nature of what can be achieved politically. Political action involves mental vulgarity, not merely because it entails the concurrence and support of those who are mentally vulgar, but because of the false simplification of human life implied in even the best of its purposes.[32]

Oakeshott's diagnosis of the ailment that beset Europe occurs, not in terms of a lack of political culture; quite the opposite, too much store is placed in the achievements of political activity. On Oakeshott's view, success in political activity goes no way toward ameliorating its necessarily abstract view of the world – if anything, political success tends to reinforce confidence in a way of understanding that is already extremely susceptible to over-confidence. Political activity is inherently flawed – it is an activity that must always fail to comprehend the full character of the order of experience to which it belongs. Oakeshott's denunciation of politics is neither based on the merely hackneyed point that politics is a hard road, nor is he concerned with the claims of particular types of regimes, with 'left-wing' or 'right-wing' movements or with 'democratic' or 'authoritarian' political arrangements. The type of claim that Oakeshott was concerned to refute is a claim about the character of political activity without further qualification.

In 'The Claims of Politics' Oakeshott fixed his sights upon a familiar assertion of the importance of political activity. It is often claimed that politics imposes a 'universal duty' to participation. This claim, Oakeshott argued, suggests 'either of two conditions … [Either] political activity [is] the only adequate expression for the communal interests of a society … or … [politics is] the most important and most effective expres-

---

[32]   *Religion, Politics and the Moral Life*, p. 93.

sion of such a sensibility ...'[33] In rejecting these positions
Oakeshott argued that political activity neither affords a complete view of the experience which it presupposes, nor is it
even the most complete view of this experience. Politics is an
abstraction of an order of experience that it can only imply
without realising, an order that generates and sustains it as a
meaningful activity. Describing politics as an abstraction
gives rise to three questions. First, what is this order of experience of which politics is an abstraction? What is the character
of the experience which politics implies but fails to fully comprehend? Second, how is abstraction manifest in political
experience? And, third, does Oakeshott's understanding of
politics allow for any positive relation between it and the experience of which it is an abstraction? Is politics merely a distortion of some more concrete experience or can it enhance and
contribute to this experience in some way?

   The first of these inquiries has already been answered in the
previous section. In 'The Claims of Politics' Oakeshott presented politics as having an abstract character:

> A political system is primarily for the protection and occa-
> sional modification of a recognized legal and social order. It is
> not self-explanatory; its end and meaning lie beyond itself in
> the social whole to which it belongs, a social whole already
> determined by law and custom and tradition, none of which is
> the creation of political activity.[34]

The social whole of which politics is an abstraction turns out to
consist of the practice of authority which, as we have seen,

---

[33] *Ibid.*, p. 91.

[34] *Ibid.*, p. 93. This position has striking parallels with the conception of
      state which led W.B. Yeats to devote himself to a national theatre in Ire-
      land before it made any sense to protect Irish culture with a political set-
      tlement. It is with this in mind that the tension between Yeats and other
      Irish nationalists can be most profitably understood. Oakeshott's famil-
      iarity and enjoyment of Yeats's poetry is evident in the many lines that
      are scattered through his essays.

Oakeshott specified in his account of the character of civil association.

Following Oakeshott's specification of the relation between civil association and politics introduces the second issue raised by his claim that politics is abstract; what is the character of this abstraction? In 'The Rule of Law' Oakeshott expressed the distinction between authority and politics as the distinction between considerations of the *lex*, or 'authenticity' (authority), of a law and considerations of the *jus*, or 'rightness' (desirability), of a law. Oakeshott's account of the relation between considerations of a law in terms of *jus* and *lex* 'entails a relationship which is at once acquiescent and critical.'[35] In considering the authoritative rules of civil association in terms of their rightness or desirability, politics exhibits a critical attitude towards these rules. This critical attitude in political activity takes the form of:

> thinking and speaking about a rule of civil intercourse which has been notionally resolved from being an authoritative prescription into a conclusion in order that what it prescribes may be distinguished from its authority and thus be made available to be considered in terms of its desirability; or it is thinking and speaking in order to reach a conclusion which may be transformed into a rule by an authoritative act.[36]

The conclusions at which political activity arrives about the rightness or desirability of a rule must always be qualified by their 'notional' character. Desirability is a notional and secondary concern in considering the character of authoritative rules. The critical aspect of political activity always acquiesces in the authority that it criticises. In questioning the desirability of a civil rule, politics must forego questioning the desirability of the comprehensive whole of civil association. The act of questioning the desirability of the comprehensive whole of

---

[35]   *On Human Conduct*, p. 164.

[36]   *Ibid.*, p. 165. Cf. 'The Vocabulary of a Modern European State', p. 287.

civil association is not an act of politics but rather an act either of secession or subversion.[37]

Oakeshott's specification of the relation between authority and political activity in 'On the Civil Condition' and 'The Rule of Law' explains his earlier declamations against politics as a limited and dangerous engagement. The limitations of political activity inhere within the character of political activity. Oakeshott understood politics as an activity that presupposes a mode of association that cannot satisfactorily be described in political terms. The notional resolutions of politics imply, without explicitly stating, the authoritative character of civil rules. Any attempt to translate the practice of civil association into political terms alone, or to reverse the priority of the authority of a civil rule by making it rely upon its desirability, results in a gross distortion of this practice. When the notional character that limits political activity is not observed, Oakeshott argued, politics challenges the practice of authority that is the very condition of its existence. Politics speaks in terms of desirability: it speaks in a persuasive idiom. But if the demonstrative or injunctive idioms of adjudication and ruling are reduced to or are seen to rest upon their ability to persuade, then civil association is reduced to voluntary association.[38] This signifies nothing less than the disappearance of civil association altogether.

The idiom of desirability in which politics speaks should not, however, be mistaken for enterprise association. Civil and enterprise modes of association are categorially distinct from one another and politics is an idiom within the authoritative language of civil association. There is nothing notional in considering enterprise rules in terms of their desirability; their desirability is the sole ground of their validity. Oakeshott

---

[37]   *On Human Conduct*, p. 164.

[38]   See *Ibid.*, pp. 173–80 and J. L. Auspitz, 'Individuality, Civility and Theory', *Political Theory*, 4 (1976) pp. 280–2.

acknowledged the vulnerability of politics to lapse into the language of enterprise association observing that political parties are 'perhaps the greatest threat to the rule of law.'[39] Political parties, associations that are themselves enterprise associations, are prone to forget the notional character of considering rules in terms of their desirability and to view rules primarily in terms of their obstruction or promotion of this or that interest or enterprise. In this circumstance 'politics' is forsaken for 'policy-management'.[40] And instead of being understood in terms of the rule of law, the state becomes understood as the 'authoritative' manager of policy or a *polizeistaat*.[41] I shall consider Oakeshott's account of the style of politics that most threatens civil association by reducing all rules to terms of desirability in greater detail in the next section.

The third issue raised by Oakeshott's claims that politics is abstract concerns whether his conception of politics allows for any positive relation between politics and the practice of authority. One could be excused for thinking that Oakeshott only ever alluded to political activity in order to denigrate it. However, he never suggested that the robustness of politics is a measure of the ill health of the practice of authority. Politics does not, on Oakeshott's understanding, appear as a blight which gains health at the expense of its host. In 'On the Civil Condition' Oakeshott described politics as 'call[ing] for so exact a focus of attention and so uncommon a self-restraint that one is not astonished to find this mode of human relationship to be as rare as it is excellent.'[42] Politics, properly understood, is an activity that best reflects the vital character of the practice of civil association, and it is to the character of civil

---

[39]   *On History*, p. 154.

[40]   See 'On the Vocabulary of a Modern European State', p. 291.

[41]   *On History*, p. 153.

[42]   *On Human Conduct*, p. 180.

rules that we must return to discover the positive function of political activity.

The compulsory character of civil rules may give them the appearance of being 'Remote, mysterious, cold and insulated alike from consent or dissent to their demands ... And it is scarcely odd that these stern but unenthusiastic ogres should be recognized as an affront to human dignity ...'[43] On Oakeshott's understanding, however, quite the opposite is the case. The authority of civil rules springs, neither from their desirability nor from their venerable or distant character, but in their being used. He insisted that 'nothing should be allowed to obscure the view of civil association as relationship in terms of a language of understanding and intercourse continuously used in conduct and enacted and re-enacted in being used'[44] and this 'practice may be modified in use, but in being used it is not used up.'[45] Oakeshott presented civil rules as the 'resources' of civil association. However, civil rules do not behave in the way resources are usually thought of.[46] When we think of using a resource we usually view it in terms of its exploitable potential. Resources are thus considered as means

---

[43]   *Ibid.*, p. 157.

[44]   *Ibid.*, p. 128. The language of enactment and re-enactment of rules does not imply that an association has motives but that civil rules are the most fundamental and comprehensive expression of civil association.

[45]   *Ibid.*, p. 121.

[46]   Cf. 'The Study of "Politics" in a University: An Essay in Appropriateness' in *Rationalism in Politics*, p. 187. 'Some people think of civilization as a stock of things like books, pictures, musical instruments and compositions, buildings, cities, landscapes, inventions, devices, machines and so on – in short, as the results of mankind having impressed itself upon a "natural world" ... The world into which we are initiated is composed, rather, of a stock of emotions, beliefs, images, ideas, manners of thinking, languages, skills, practices and manners of activity out of which "things" are generated. And consequently it is appropriate to think of it not as a stock but as a capital; that is, something to be enjoyed only in use ... And in use it earns an interest, part of which is consumed in a current manner of living and part reinvested.'

to ends and they diminish in the degree to which they are successfully exploited in advancing ends. But the resources of
civil association do not behave in this way. The scope of civil
rules increases as they are used. They are used when they are
understood to qualify the performances that agents choose. As
civil rules are used they may acquire fresh nuances which tend
in hitherto unexplored directions.[47] And, on falling out of use
the moral practices that provide the context of civil rules ossify
or evaporate. Under such circumstances civil rules become
anachronisms.

Civil association is a practice and as such bears all the characteristics of a tradition that Oakeshott elucidated in some of
the essays of *Rationalism in Politics.* [48] So, Oakeshott found in
civil association:

> the work of local human intelligences ... recognized to com-
> pose a more or less coherent system of rules. But considering
> the provenance of any such system of rules and the circum-
> stances in which it was put together, it cannot be expected to
> display any notable elegance or economy of design; nor can it
> escape being ragged at the edges, intimating situations to
> which it has no precise response.[49]

Furthermore, civil rules are 'never more than a very imperfect reflection of what are believed to be "just" conditions of
conduct ...'[50] Civil rules are not static precepts carved in gran-
ite; they exist through being used. And as the way that the
members of an association disclose their beliefs in conduct
change (no two performances subscribe to a practice in exactly
the same way), so particular rules become irrelevant and fade

---

[47]   For example, *On Human Conduct*, p. 136, 'If a hole in a fence large enough
       for a child to squeeze through has been declared a circumstance which
       may transform an infant intruder from a trespasser to an invitee, what is
       to be said about a gate without a latch in respect of an adult?'

[48]   See Auspitz, 'Individuality, Civility and Theory', pp. 273–6.

[49]   *On Human Conduct*, p. 177.

[50]   *Ibid.*, p. 154.

from the scene. Rules that have been enacted in legislation are repealed and new rules introduced. And a tradition dies when it is no longer used, appealed to or remembered.

The always unfinished and often incoherent condition of civil rules requires that they be considered in terms of their appropriateness, rightness or effectiveness, in short their desirability, and this is the proper sphere of politics. Oakeshott offered an example of political activity in the enfranchisement of women in Britain:

> the legal status of women in our society was for a long time (and perhaps still is) in comparative confusion, because the rights and duties which composed it intimate rights and duties which were nevertheless not recognized ... the only cogent reason to be advanced for the technical 'enfranchisement' of women was that in all or most other important respects they had already been enfranchised ... Arguments drawn from abstract natural right ... or some other general concept of feminine personality, must be regarded ... as irrelevant ... the one valid argument ... [is] that there was an incoherence in the arrangements of the society which pressed convincingly for remedy.[51]

The changed and changing position of women after electoral enfranchisement cannot be explained by arguing that society had somehow become aware of their natural right to vote – it might as well have recognised the natural right of bowlers to throw the ball in cricket matches![52] Oakeshott understood the technical enfranchisement of women as resulting from a myriad of contingent happenings in society. It does not constitute a fresh step taken in the inexorable march of progress toward whichever of its alleged destinations. It comes as the result of pursuing a particular set of intimations that were already afoot. On this reading progress has no single

---

[51]   *Rationalism in Politics*, p. 57.
[52]   *Ibid.*, p. 68.

destination; one is always, more or less, in transit. In Oakeshott's famous image of 'political activity, then, men sail a boundless and bottomless sea; there is neither harbour for shelter nor floor for anchorage, neither starting place nor appointed destination.'[53]

Some critics have argued that Oakeshott's reasoning could as easily justify the total disenfranchisement of women, thus re-establishing coherence in their social condition.[54] But, the fact that Oakeshott believed that there is no external authority in civil association does not mean that civil association may remain deaf and blind to the tensions and incoherencies that rise to the surface in the enactments and re-enactments of these rules. He wrote of tradition that it 'is not blind, it is only "blind as a bat."'[55] If politics is about keeping the practice of civil association afloat, then it is an activity that must be awake to demands which, if they go unacknowledged, run the risk of sinking the ship. Simply to deny that women are educated, that they play an economically significant role in the community and asserting that they are incapable of exercising political responsibility on account of being women, would have made for an intolerable situation. To disenfranchise a section of the community which is, in fact, already enfranchised and busy exploring the possibilities in their franchise must work at cross purposes to anything which political activity has to offer by way of maintaining the relevance of civil rules. Nor does this mean that political activity must always *follow* fashions and trends already astir: 'a lively political imagination may recognize [changes in circumstance] before they are half over the moral horizon.'[56]

---

[53]   *Ibid.*, p. 60.

[54]   D.D. Raphael, 'Professor Oakeshott's *Rationalism in Politics*', *Political Studies*, 12 (1964), p. 213.

[55]   *Rationalism in Politics*, p. 471.

[56]   *On Human Conduct*, p. 180.

Oakeshott was, then, both apprehensive and admiring of political activity. He was apprehensive of politics because it is an abstract activity, which is prone to forget its abstract character. Politics has a tendency to become carried away with its accomplishments and prospects demanding service from that which it should be serving. If the abstract character of politics is forgotten and the notional quality of the conclusions that politics makes about the desirability of civil rules is ignored, then politics may destroy the very conditions of its existence and a state of civil war (a misnomer if ever there was one) has supervened upon civil association. Oakeshott's apprehensiveness at politics constitutes one of the many echoes in his writings of Thomas Hobbes, who witnessed some of the worst excesses of an over-inflated faith in politics experienced in modern Britain. Hobbes responded to the excesses of his time by arguing for conditions that would tame political activity and aspirations in some cases to the point of extinction.[57] Oakeshott's apprehensiveness at political excess was, perhaps, not so deep as that of Hobbes's. I think that Oakeshott's conception of politics would allow that the English civil wars resulted as much from the rigidity of Charles in political matters (and this is perhaps true of all the Stuarts) as from the excessive expectations of Parliament. Oakeshott insisted on the necessary place of politics in the practice of authority and was suitably impressed by instances of it being conducted with due propriety.

Attending to Oakeshott's account of politics brings to the fore the character of civil association as a current practice that can change without losing its identity. The principle of identity is recognised in its authoritative character but authority is not exclusive of consideration of specific rules in terms of their

---

[57]   One example of Hobbes's suspicion of politics is his preference for monarchy, presumably, because deliberation (politics) is confined within the single natural person of the monarch rather than an artificial person consisting of many natural persons.

desirability. In acknowledging the secondary but important character of the desirability of civil rules, the practice of civil association is able to accommodate the ever-changing circumstances in which agents understand themselves and the choices they make in responding to these circumstances without suffering dissipation. Against the backdrop of civil association, a myriad of enterprise associations may proliferate and, Oakeshott believed, civil association to be at its safest when there are many enterprise associations.[58] When the desirability of conditions is considered as their primary quality, enterprise association has prevailed to the exclusion of all other modes of association. (Enterprise associations that do not pretend to be compulsory do not fall into this category.)

3. The Politics of Faith and the Politics of Scepticism

I have argued that Oakeshott exhibited an ambiguous attitude towards political activity. On the one hand, he was apprehensive of politics because it is by its very character a limited activity that has a propensity to ignore its limited character. On the other hand, he found politics to be a necessary and admirable achievement when it overcomes the temptation to ignore its limited character. Oakeshott's apprehensiveness at political activity reached a high point in his denunciations of it in 'The Claims of Politics'. In this essay his vigorous protestations at the over-importance attributed to politics are hardly qualified by his brief attendance upon its positive function:

> Nothing I have said should be taken to mean that I think political action is a wholly valueless expression of a sensibility for the communal interests of a society; in my view it is a legiti-

---

[58]   See Oakeshott's account of the importance of the freedom of association in 'The Political Economy of Freedom' published in *Rationalism in Politics*, pp. 384–406.

mate expression, and one which it is impossible for a society to go without.[59]

Composed against a backdrop of tumultuous political events, at a time when politics was laying claim to ever greater areas of activity, Oakeshott was concerned, first and foremost, to warn against the dangers of these claims.

Oakeshott's view of the ambiguous (rather than the merely dangerous) character of politics becomes more apparent in a number of works written after 'The Claims of Politics'. He explored the features of the morality of the individual and the morality of the anti-individual most thoroughly in terms of their respective conceptions of the proper office of government, and considering the proper office of government is a political consideration. 'The Masses in Representative Democracy', *The Harvard Lectures* and 'On the Character of a Modern European State' each identify distinct conceptions of the proper office of government that emerged in the service of the morality of the individual and the morality of the anti-individual. Oakeshott distinguished between these respective conceptions of the office of government as 'parliamentary democracy' and 'popular democracy', 'the political theory of individualism' and 'the political theory of collectivism' and 'politics' and 'policy-management'.[60]

Oakeshott's most extended account of the ambiguous character of the office of government in the modern European state was composed in the 1950s and has been published posthumously under the title *The Politics of Faith and the Politics of Scepticism*. Before exploring his characterisation of the politics of faith and the politics of scepticism, however, we should be

[59] *Religion, Politics and the Moral Life*, p. 94.

[60] Oakeshott refers to 'parliamentary and popular democracy' in 'The Masses in Representative Democracy', 'the political theories of individualism and collectivism' in *The Harvard Lectures* and 'politics and policy-management' in 'On the Civil Condition', 'On the Character of a Modern European State' and 'The Rule of Law'.

clear as to what precisely these terms refer. The politics of faith and the politics of scepticism do not denote modes of association; they do not refer to the constitution of association but rather to the proper office of government: that is, 'What shall government (composed and authorized in whatever manner we think proper) do?'[61] The politics of faith and the politics of scepticism do, however, imply distinct conceptions of the constitution of a state, which Oakeshott characterised as *societas* and *universitas* in 'On the Character of a Modern European State.'[62]

Oakeshott's politics of faith and politics of scepticism imply distinct assumptions about the character of the activity of governing. On the one hand, a politics of faith assumes

> a single path to perfection or improvement, no matter how slowly you are prepared to move along it … you are a perfectionist, not because you know in detail what is at the end, but because you have excluded every other road and are content with the certainty that perfection lies wherever it leads. And the office given to government in this enterprise is appropriate not only because of the amount of power it can exert but also because it needs to be exerted in one direction only.[63]

The assumption of a single way to perfection or improvement is reflected in an understanding of 'governing as an "unlimited" activity; government is omnicompetent.'[64] The omnicompetence of government assumed in a politics of faith entails that government has a duty to be always 'at the end of its tether', concerning itself as far as possible in the minutiae of

---

[61]   *The Politics of Faith and the Politics of Scepticism*, p. 3. Cf. *On Human Conduct*, p. 193 and *The Harvard Lectures*, pp. 9–12.

[62]   *Societas* and *universitas* are historical analogues of civil and enterprise modes of association.

[63]   *The Politics of Faith and the Politics of Scepticism*, p. 26.

[64]   *Ibid.*, p. 27.

the activities of those it governs.[65] On the other hand, a politics of scepticism assumes that 'to pursue perfection in one direction only … is to invite disappointment and (what might be worse than the mortification of non-arrival) misery on the way.'[66] A politics of scepticism, then, 'deprives the activity of governing of the comprehensive purpose … In this understanding of politics … the activity of governing subsists not because it is good, but because it is necessary. Its chief office is to lessen the severity of human conflict by reducing the occasion of it.'[67] A politics of faith assumes a single human condition and a single condition of perfection that are sundered one from the other by circumstance, and that it is within human capability to overcome the adversity of circumstance. A politics of scepticism maintains the human condition is its circumstance and while various elements of this condition may be ameliorated, we cannot be fully relieved of it in this life.

A politics of faith and a politics of scepticism may arrive at similar conclusions about the desirability or undesirability of a particular situation but they do so on very different grounds. Oakeshott found an apparent point of concurrence of the politics of faith and the politics of scepticism in seventeenth century English puritanism;

> The politics of English puritanism appeared first as the politics of opposition; and what was opposed was the current government and in particular its ecclesiastical settlement. This could be opposed from either of two points of view: because any general settlement which imposed a uniform system was objected to [Brownists, Congregationalists and Independents]; or because a uniform system was desired, but not this

---

[65]   *Ibid.*, p. 74.

[66]   *Ibid.*, p. 31.

[67]   *Ibid.*, p. 32.

one because it is identified as error [Presbyterians and Fifth Monarchists].[68]

And, when the term 'democracy' is understood as describing, not the constitution of a state or who should govern, but the proper office of government,

> it may mean either government turned in the direction of faih or it may mean government turned in the direction of scepticism … If the manner is that of faith, then 'institutions' are understood solely in respect of the power with which they are able to endow government, and the virtue of 'popular' institutions is recognized to be their capacity to provide government with greater quantities of power than any other … If, on the other hand, the manner is that of scepticism, then the 'institutions' we are considering are understood principally in respect of their ability to control government …[69]

Thus the politics of faith and the politics of scepticism are responsible for an ambiguity that infects the political vocabulary of modern Europe so deeply that 'it would be difficult to find a single word that is not double-tongued or a single conception which is not double-edged.'[70] Oakeshott's politics of faith and politics of scepticism describe two poles, between which political experience in Europe has vacillated over the last five centuries. European political experience has rarely reached one of these poles and then only ever for an instant. For arrival at one pole, (which entails the complete exclusion of the other) is a self-defeating accomplishment.

Oakeshott argued that the modern European political experience is complex and to suggest that a single element in this complexity could survive the complete absence of the other is to suggest that the modern European political experience is more or less than it is. In modern Europe the politics of faith

[68] *Ibid.*, pp. 59–60.

[69] *Ibid.*, p. 131.

[70] *Ibid.*, p. 13.

and the politics of scepticism have shared an uncomfortable partnership, 'as a rule where faith is a wife, scepticism is a mistress; and the lover of scepticism will be found also to be the friend of faith.'[71] The depiction of the politics of faith and the politics of scepticism as a partnership pre-empts Oakeshott's formulation of the relationship between the conceptions of the modern European state as *societas* and *universitas* of over two decades later: 'each is a historic character and a character on the wing continuously exposed to modification in intercourse with the other. In a modern European state they are not friends but neither are they exactly foes; perhaps, as was said of England and France in the sixteenth century, their relationship is that of "sweet enemies"'.[72]

Oakeshott's account of the self-defeat inherent in the destruction of the complex character of politics can be outlined in terms of its corruption of the proper relation between authority and desirability in the practice of civil association. He argued that the politics of faith is self-defeating on three grounds. First, the politics of faith, if unchecked by scepticism, attributes political significance to every activity so that 'What exists (for example) is not "football", but "football-in-so-far-as-it-promotes-perfection" ...'[73] All activity is considered significant only in its promotion of perfection, so that all activity is politically significant. If all activity is understood as political activity, if all citizens are agents of the government, then there is no need of government because there are no subjects to govern. As a result, 'When government is understood as an activity of limitless control, it finds itself with nothing to control ...'[74] Governments that have proceeded down this path have always found an external enemy within, 'the unre-

---

[71]   *Ibid.*, p. 59.

[72]   *On Human Conduct*, p. 326.

[73]   *The Politics of Faith and the Politics of Scepticism*, p. 93.

[74]   *Ibid.*, p. 49.

generate', 'idleness', 'agents of the bourgeoisie', 'communist provocateurs' and so on, who have provided an excuse for vigilant government. But this describes a situation of war rather than politics. The notional character of politics is replaced with the substantive activity of policy-management and the replacement of politics with policy-management is indicative of enterprise association having supplanted civil association and a morality of the anti-individual having prevailed over a morality of the individual.

The second ground on which Oakeshott argued that an uninhibited politics of faith is self-defeating also follows from the totalitarian aspirations of this style of politics when unfettered by scepticism:

> the more power [government] acquires, and indeed the more successful it appears in subduing the diverse activities to one activity, the more closely it will come to resemble an alien authority, until in the end it reveals itself (in respect of its power and its hostility) as a "force of nature". And a people whose activity is being directed, and being ever more thoroughly directed ... will recognize such a force as something it has been taught to oppose, or at least outwit. Thus ... the politics of faith ... may be seen to defeat itself by adding one more direction of activity to the already multiple directions, namely, the search for imprecisions in the pattern, the profitless activity of circumventing the minute control it is endeavouring to impose.[75]

Government comes to resemble an alien authority – its power is authorised, not in the intrinsic terms of civil association but in terms of an extrinsic purpose. In intimating enterprise association, a politics of faith cannot avoid (even if it insists on denying) that this mode of association presupposes, at the very least, one other condition, that is, the condition of not being associated in the enterprise. As a particular enter-

---

[75] *Ibid.*, p. 95.

prise comes to dominate the association, whether by coercion or by consent, non-participation in the enterprise will increasingly become the condition of all other activity.

The first two of Oakeshott's arguments for the self-defeating character of the politics of faith concerned the extension of the office of government to its zenith. The character of this extension is spatial in the sense that no area of activity is acknowledged as legitimate that does not contribute to the activity of governing. The third ground on which Oakeshott argued that the politics of faith is self-defeating differs from the first two in that it refers to the temporal assumptions which underlie this style of government's view of perfection. He observed that the politics of faith in modern Europe has been manifest in a rich variety of undertakings. The politics of faith has promoted a diverse set of enterprises. Instances can be found in the many recipes for the promotion of wealth, the re-distribution of this wealth and the many attempts to found or prepare the way for a New Jerusalem by imposing an austere 'rule of saints'.[76] The diversity and apparent incompatibility of these projects with one another belies the formal similarity of their conceptions of perfection:

> each belong[s] to a particular historic context, and it is this context which gives them their specific character and plausibility. But in the politics of faith the exclusive conditions must be pursued as if its validity were permanent, not merely historical. Everything in this style of government is built to last; where the design of "perfection" has been discovered change need neither be feared nor anticipated ...[77]

A politics of faith leaves no room for the on-going qualification of its conception of perfection by historical circumstance. The way to perfection lies, and has always lain, along a single path which exists untouched by the vicissitudes of contin-

---

[76] See *The Harvard Lectures*, Lectures 7 and 8.

[77] *The Politics of Faith and the Politics of Scepticism*, p. 96.

gency. In some versions of the politics of faith, perfection is presented as the *telos* of history, but history in these instances is understood to involve the operation of 'iron laws of necessity' or some equivalent device. On this understanding, history is itself reduced to the pursuit of perfection in a single direction.

The ahistorical view of perfection bears out two consequences for the politics of faith. The first refers to the propensity of the politics of faith to mistake the character of civil association for enterprise association and the second reveals the shortcomings of enterprise association in securing any meaningful condition of perfection. The first consequence of the ahistorical character of perfection assumed in a politics of faith is its adverse impact upon the practice of civil association. Oakeshott observed that civil rules are the resources of civil association. Civil rules are, however, resources of an unusual sort, for in being used they are not used up. Civil rules are not used up in being used precisely because they exist in the present – they arise from on-going, non-instrumental practices. A politics of faith has no need for association in terms of on-going rules because the whole enterprise in this style of government is to arrive. Rules are, then, of value only in so far as they promote perfection; they are either instrumental devices or hindrances and distractions. Thus, in the politics of faith:

> a high degree of formality in the activity of governing would be out of character ... a nice observance of rules and constitutions will readily be felt to hinder its impetus. Rights, the means of redress, will be incongruous, their place being taken by a single, comprehensive Right – the right to participate in the improvement which leads to perfection ... the present will be more important than the past, and the future [more important] than either ... prevention will be considered better than punishment; that the innocent should suffer will appear less

vile than that the guilty should escape, and guilt will more
readily be presumed than innocence.[78]

In short, the politics of faith divines the authority to govern
from an idea of perfection that lies beyond association.[79] Civil
association is viewed not as an on-going practice but as an
expendable resource whose only value is to be exploited for
future perfection and improvement. In reducing the authority
of civil rules to considerations of their desirability enterprise
association has, once again, prevailed over civil association.

The second consequence which follows from the ahistorical
character of perfection assumed in the politics of faith reveals
the unsatisfactory character of perfection that is available
within the politics of faith and in enterprise association. Perfection, in the politics of faith, appears sure and the path certain because the direction is known even if the terrain over
which the path travels is not. The pursuit of perfection as a permanent condition, when undertaken (as it must be) in an
ever-changing world, can only emphasise the impermanent
character of perfection. Thus Oakeshott found 'the imperish-
able monuments of the politics of faith are [in fact] imperish-
able ruins, "follies" remarkable often for the strength of their
materials and always for the eccentricity of their design.'[80]
The assembled aspirations and achievements of the politics of
faith amount to a museum display boasting an impressive
array of curiosities: Savonarola's Florence and Calvin's
Geneva, Fourier's *phalanxes* and Bacon's New Atlantis, Marx's
dictatorship of the proletariat, Hitler's Third Reich and

---

[78] *Ibid.,* p. 29. The addition in parenthesis is made by the editor.

[79] Although, Oakeshott points out, 'the chosen direction may impose itself
      gradually, or it may be imposed in a revolutionary manner. But what-
      ever the manner of its appearance and imposition, it is unavoidably one
      of the directions of activity already intimated in the society upon which
      it is to be imposed: government, in this style of politics, is never the
      imposition of an entirely fresh direction of activity.' *Ibid.,* p. 93.

[80] *Ibid.,* p. 96.

Owen's New Lannark, to note but a few. In surveying this archaeological site of past (and current) dreams, one is reminded of the irony in the inscription left by Shelley's empire-builder; 'Look on my works, ye mighty and despair.'[81] The politics of faith exhibit a consistent propensity to supplant civil association with enterprise association; to overthrow considerations of authority with considerations of desirability. Desire cannot, however, deliver unconditional perfection. We may recall, once again, the observation of Hobbes, that felicity, when understood as the satisfaction of a substantive desire, can never realise perfection. The satisfaction of a desire is fatal to that desire and it is almost immediately supplanted by another in an endless train of desires, or the desire is never supplanted and either fades or remains unfulfilled. If an enterprise is one amongst many, all is not lost when the goal is either achieved or irretrievably lost – there are other enterprises waiting to be explored; but when there is only a single enterprise all is lost if the goal is lost and there would be an inevitable loss of purpose in the unnerving event that the goal of perfection is achieved.[82]

The politics of scepticism, like the politics of faith, also exhibits a self-defeating character when it dominates the political stage to the complete exclusion of its partner. Oakeshott began his account of the self-defeat inherent in the politics of scepticism with a qualification; 'The nemesis of sceptical politics, when they are freed from any modifying agency, is less spectacular than that of the politics of faith … the self-defeat of scepticism is both less devastating and more subtle.'[83] Self-defeat in the politics of scepticism is less devastating because this style of government is less extreme than the poli-

---

[81] P.B. Shelley, 'Ozymandias', *The Complete Works of Percy Bysshe Shelley*, (ed. T. Hutchinson) (London, Oxford University Press, 1948), p. 550.

[82] See 'The Tower of Babel' in *On History*.

[83] *The Politics of Faith and the Politics of Scepticism*, p. 105.

tics of faith. The politics of faith calls for maximum government, whereas the politics of scepticism calls, not for no government, but for minimum government.[84] Far from promoting anarchy, the politics of scepticism understands government to have 'a positive office, the maintenance of a relevant public order … and it can rise above minimum government, and be imperial in its own province, without approximating itself to rule in the manner of faith.'[85] However, the root of self-defeat inherent in the politics of scepticism is its inability or unwillingness to appreciate the occasions that call for it to act imperially either within or, on rare occasions, outside its normal sphere. The politics of scepticism holds that 'there can be no emergency: where the law is at the mercy of occasion there is an end to the rule of law; and where modifications in the systems of rights and duties are in response to extraordinary circumstances, they may introduce a temporary and local appropriateness but only at the cost of damaging the whole fabric which it is the office of government to protect.'[86]

The reticence of the politics of scepticism to acknowledge conditions of emergency reveals a self-defeating character on two levels. On the first level Oakeshott observed that modern European societies are characterised by particularly high levels of 'energy and enterprise'. Modern Europe consists of societies that are made up of a great diversity of enterprises pursued with an unusually high level of energy. A politics of scepticism allows this energy and enterprise to develop in as

---

[84]   *Ibid.*, p. 114, 'If the politics of scepticism represented mere anarchy, then this style of government would be inherently self-contradictory, and would be as fully dependent upon faith as in fact faith is upon it: anarchy and faith, when they stand alone, are each, in different manners, the abolition of "government". But scepticism is not anarchy; it is not even disposed to anarchy. And in virtue of its escape from anarchy it escapes inherent self-destruction as a manner of government.'

[85]   *Ibid.*, p. 106.

[86]   *Ibid.*, p. 108.

many ways as it will while restricting, as far as possible, different directions of activity from interfering with one another. So sceptical politics retards activity in a society that values vigour and enthusiasm and thus it appears out of step with the very conditions that make it necessary: 'Not to be readily understood by its subjects is, for a style of government, to be convicted of inappropriateness … [The politics of scepticism] abdicates exactly at the point where the activist expects an assertion of authority; it withdraws where he expects it to proceed; it insists upon technicalities; it is narrow severe and unenthusiastic; it is without courage or conviction.'[87] The passage recalls Yeats's lament:

> The best lack all conviction, while the worst
> Are full of passionate intensity.[88]

Yeats was all too aware of the propensity of politics to suffer the excesses of a deluded faith in its own abilities; a propensity that he took to task on more than one occasion, but he also noticed the shortcomings of another disposition so out of touch with its time that it refuses to defend itself or the body politic to which it belongs. The first ground of self-defeat in Oakeshott's account of the politics of scepticism is, then, its apparent inappropriateness. The conditions of a vigorous and enthusiastic body politic, which make this style of government so necessary, also condemn it as an activity that makes what is commonly understood as a virtue into a vice. In the absence of the modifying influence of the politics of faith, the politics of scepticism appears senescent, rambling and purposeless in a world full to the brim with youthful vitality and enthusiasm.

The second level of self-defeat inherent within the politics of scepticism is far more serious than the first. At this level the

[87]   *Ibid.,* p. 109.

[88]   W.B. Yeats, 'The Second Coming', *Michael Robartes and the Dancer*, (1921) in the *Collected Poems of W.B. Yeats*, (London, Mamillan, 1978), p. 211.

self-defeat of the politics of scepticism is not merely circumstantial, it is inherent in the partial character of its understanding of politics. In arguing this point Oakeshott re-formulated the politics of faith and the politics of scepticism as, on the one hand, the disposition to be earnest and, on the other, the disposition to play.[89] The politics of scepticism arises in a disposition to play and

> By play, I mean activity pursued on certain specific occasions, at fixed times and in a place set apart and according to exact rules; the significance of the activity lying not in a terminal result aimed at, but in the disposition which is enjoyed and fostered in the cause of the activity.[90]

Play conveys a limited character to activity that is wholly in keeping with the politics of scepticism.

Oakeshott contrasted the disposition to play with the disposition to be earnest, that is, '"serious" activity or with what might be called "ordinary life".'[91] He added that 'whenever we insist upon the manner rather than the result we are, in this sense, "at play".'[92] If the politics of scepticism is left entirely to its own devices, the manner in which the activity is carried out becomes the only consideration. Even the terms of a game are more than just the manner in which the activity is carried out – in a game a sense of play is essential but

> The self-defeat of 'play' is the lethargy which overtakes the game when one of the players is wholly indifferent about winning … In 'play' properly speaking, victory and defeat are irrelevant; but without the illusion that winning matters,

---

[89]   *The Politics of Faith and the Politics of Scepticism*, p. 112.

[90]   *Ibid.*, p. 110.

[91]   *Ibid.*

[92]   *Ibid.*, p. 111.

'play' is impossible. This is the nemesis of 'play': the belief that
there is *nothing* serious in mortality.[93]

Unmodified by the politics of faith, politics loses its impetus
towards the excessive claims that fuelled Oakeshott's apprehensiveness at this activity. Politics is, however, also a necessary function within civil association. To deprive civil
association of politics by reducing it to pure play inhibits the
on-going and vital character of civil rules. In being used, civil
rules disclose hitherto unexplored and often unexpected
directions, directions not necessarily consistent with other
directions currently afoot in association and not necessarily
consistent with existing arrangements. Politics is not a device
by which the vital qualities of civil association are dissipated
and the status quo maintained; it is an activity that maintains
the relevance of civil rules to the life of association. Without a
healthy political culture, civil association ceases to be relevant,
civil rules fall out of use and in this circumstance, the practice
of authority is destroyed.

Oakeshott's account of the politics of faith and the politics of
scepticism drives home the unsustainable conception of the
state in terms of enterprise association. When a politics of faith
prevails completely, unhindered by scepticism, enterprise
association replaces civil association and a morality of the
anti-individual has supervened upon the course of events.
Oakeshott's formulation of the principles of association in
terms of the authority and desirability of prescribed conditions echoes the distinct conceptions of salvation intimated in
the morality of the individual and the morality of the anti-individual. Authority as a principle of association refers to a current practice that accepts the necessity of accommodating
change while maintaining an identity within each moment.
Considering conditions in terms of their desirability bears out
characteristics of the conception of salvation intimated in the

---

[93] *Ibid.*, p. 113.

morality of the anti-individual. The politics of faith exhibits a faith in salvation in this world, not however in the present order of things but in another order that can be obtained. Humanity finds itself in an imperfect situation but the situation is salvageable. Salvation lies not in the present, or a reconciliation to nothingness, but in a future order for which present sacrifices are called. The present is to be sacrificed for a future hope.

Chapter 5

Poetic Experience

Sensibility, Autonomy and the Collective Dream

Exploring Oakeshott's characterisation of poetic experience to discern a general purpose to life as a whole, Lewis's third class of moral consideration, assumes a quite controversial position for two reasons. First, Oakeshott's writings are hostile to any suggestion that life has a general purpose if the purpose is presented in terms of a common substantive condition or end for humanity.[1] The idea of a substantive condition common to all humanity, 'where not only is there one law for the lion and the ox but the lion shall eat straw like the ox', is anathema to Oakeshott's account of conduct.[2] However, Oakeshott left open the possibility of referring to humanity in terms of a general purpose that could be discerned in the formal aspect of conduct. Second, the suggestion that a purpose general to life can be found in Oakeshott's account of poetic experience con-

---

[1]   For instance, *On Human Conduct* pp. 54 and 118, note 1.

[2]   Oakeshott, *Rationalism in Politics*, p. 297.

tradicts the central tenet of his most concerted and well-known work on aesthetics, 'The Voice of Poetry in the Conversation of Mankind'. In 'The Voice of Poetry', Oakeshott argued that the world of poetic experience is autonomous from other worlds of experience including the world of conduct. The following chapter surveys Oakeshott's references to the character poetry and argues that, when the entire body of his writings is taken into account, his position on the character of poetic experience is far more ambiguous than if we focus exclusively upon 'The Voice of Poetry'. In this vein, Grant (who is one of the first commentators upon Oakeshott's work to consider his account of poetry at any length) argued that: 'For Oakeshott, in the end, Poetry remains ambiguous, paradoxical and plural.'[3] Grant's five page consideration of Oakeshott's characterisation of poetic experience and its relation to moral and religious idioms within the world of conduct is one of the best presentations of the little that has been published on the subject.[4] It falls far short, however, of a comprehensive survey and treatment of its topic.

The publication of 'The Voice of Poetry' in *Rationalism in Politics* marks the only occasion on which Oakeshott explicitly disavowed himself of a former position. In the preface to this work he explained the inclusion of 'the essay on poetry [as] a belated retraction of a foolish sentence in *Experience and Its Modes*.'[5] I shall come to the so-called 'foolish sentence' in due course. For the moment it will do to notice that this 'remarkable volte-face', as Grant called it, is remarkable, not only in registering the sole instance of such an explicit repudiation of a previous position, but also because it implies that there is only

---

[3]   Grant, *Oakeshott*, p. 109.

[4]   Also see N.K. O'Sullivan, *The Problem of Political Obligation in the Writings of T.H. Green, B. Bosanquet and M. Oakeshott*, (New York, Garland, 1987), pp. 261–9.

[5]   *Rationalism in Politics*, p. xi.

one position to repudiate, which consisted in a single, throwaway sentence.[6] The scattered references to poetry in Oakeshott's work, both before and after 'The Voice of Poetry', show this to be far from the case. Oakeshott expressed views about the relation of poetic experience to religion and morality on more than one occasion, and these views are neither clear nor are they clearly consistent with one another. At times he distinguished categorially between poetic and religious experience but, for the most part, he implied that they share a somewhat closer but unspecified relation.

The first section of the following chapter outlines Oakeshott's account of religion and poetry as sensibility. Oakeshott's early interest in poetic experience and its place in the world of conduct is far more substantial than is implied in his later dismissal of a foolish sentence in *Experience and Its Modes* and, in fact, remains evident in some passages in *On Human Conduct*. I conclude the first section by finding the root of two inconsistent views of poetic experience in *Experience and Its Modes* that becomes increasingly pronounced in his later works. Section two traces one pole of this ambiguity in the gradual development of Oakeshott's arguments for the autonomy of poetic experience, in particular from the world of conduct. Section three traces the other pole of this ambiguity in Oakeshott's outline of a poetic experience as intimating a condition common to humanity and suggests a general purpose may be drawn from this common condition.

1. Poetic Experience as Sensibility

The first publication in which Oakeshott considered the character of poetry is a little known essay, published in the Gonville and Caius College magazine, entitled 'Shylock the

---

[6]   Grant, *Oakeshott*, p. 104.

Jew: An Essay in Villainy'.[7] In this essay he described the 'out-standing quality' of artists as their capacity to sympathise with their characters: 'Sympathy does not imply any absolute moral standard; in fact it requires a casting aside of all precon-ceptions which may colour our judgement, so that we may, so far as possible, be *at one* with him whom we wish to know.'[8] The artist and the audience whom the artist addresses must put to one side their moral prejudices so that they may appre-ciate a dramatic character as 'a picture painted from the inside.'[9] Oakeshott distinguished between morally judging and poetically appreciating a character but he went no further. He was not undertaking a philosophical consideration of the relation between the worlds of poetic experience and conduct but rather arguing that, as a dramatic image, Shylock appears as a more comprehensive character than when he is viewed in terms of the moral prejudices by which we judge our own con-duct and the conduct of others.

To find in Shylock only a moral caricature of 'the Jew' – greed for worldly riches and so on – is to miss a crucial quality in his character. Besides this worldly aspect, Shylock is also 'a proud man, a man with many good qualities whose misfor-tune it is to be judged, not on his own merits, but on the prover-bial character of his race.'[10] Oakeshott found in Shakespeare's character 'a constant state of vibration [and] fluctuation throughout the play.'[11] The extremes that describe the limits of Shylock's character are, on the one hand, a nobility of pride in his religion and his cultural inheritance and, on the other, a base concern for material wealth. Neither extreme completely

---

[7]   M. Oakeshott, 'Shylock the Jew: An Essay in Villainy', *The Caian*, 30 (Michaelmas, 1921).

[8]   *Ibid.*, p. 63.

[9]   *Ibid.*

[10]   *Ibid.*, p. 64.

[11]   *Ibid.*, p. 65.

dominates his character but each appears, at different moments, in different degrees of intensity. For Oakeshott, the genius of Shakespeare is his creation of characters who are full and dynamic of themselves; 'they must ... be able to exist apart [from a background of other moral characters], even if such an existence were uncongenial.'[12] So, considered solely as a moral allegory, Shylock is less than a full character. Oakeshott did not, of course, deny the worldly aspect of Shakespeare's character but insists that, if Shylock is to be fully appreciated as a dramatic character, then his worldly presence must be taken together with his nobility of pride.

Four years after the publication of 'Shylock', Oakeshott referred again to poetic contemplation in relation to the moral life. In 'Some Remarks Concerning the Nature and Meaning of Sociality', he argued that poetic contemplation, far from opposing morality, is exemplary of the type of sociality experienced in solitude: 'It may be with books, it often is with the great figures of history and of poetry that such a man finds his life. And this life of imagination is a thousand times more social than the common life of the majority of people ... '[13] Here, it is quite clearly the act of contemplation, and not the subject contemplated, that constitutes the experience of sociality; the poetic appreciation of sociality in solitude 'is seen, perhaps, at its greatest in Wordsworth who finds satisfaction in "nature" simply because of his deep imaginative sense of the unity of things ... '[14] As manifestations of sociality, poetic and religious experience are analogous to one another; 'In society, a meal is no longer merely a means of satisfying hunger ... The trivial objects which grace the board have a poetic religious and moral significance which, present indeed at every meal, is found at its highest when religion, as it so

---

[12]   *Ibid.*, p. 62.

[13]   *Religion, Politics and the Moral Life*, p. 54.

[14]   *Ibid.*, pp. 54–5.

often has done, makes them the centre of the intensest social unity.'[15] When a meal is understood as an act of communion with one's fellows and one's God, it takes on a significance that is at once poetic, religious and moral. Oakeshott appeared to make no distinction between poetic, religious and moral experience on this occasion and the impression of this indistinctness is confirmed in *Some Matters Preliminary* when he identified 'a father bringing his son up to appreciate poetry [as] an action of the State … '[16] While Oakeshott may have had in mind some sort of non-specific distinction between poetry, religion and morality (at least in name), their common character as expressions of sociality or the State is far more significant than any quality which might distinguish them from one another.

Poetic and religious experience are, then, both idioms of sociality in which experience is elevated above the mundane level of everyday conduct. Oakeshott pressed home the concrete character of poetic and religious experience in 'Religion and the World', when he likened the enactment of a religious self to the creativity of youth in which 'The length of art does not dismay us, for we are not conscious of the shortness of life. Indeed this discrepancy between the length of art and that of life is altogether false, depending as it does, upon the world's notion that art is to be found in galleries and libraries or anywhere except in a personal sensibility.'[17] Again, Oakeshott did not necessarily reduce art to the religious life but the essence of both poetic and religious experience lies in sensibility rather than the external trappings of great art collections or the mere symbols of piety. Oakeshott's distinction between religious and worldly systems of value in 'Religion and the World' echoes his earlier distinction between poetic appreciation and

---

[15] *Ibid.,* p. 57.

[16] *Some Matters Preliminary,* p. 154.

[17] *Religion, Politics and the Moral Life,* p. 34.

moral judgement in 'Shylock'. A religious system of value, like a dramatic image, arises when a character is understood from the inside; and a worldly system of value, like the caricature of moral prejudice, springs from the representation of a character that is only skin deep.

The analogous character of poetic and religious experience is maintained in *Experience and Its Modes*. Oakeshott presented 'The most thoroughly and positively practical life is that of the artist or the mystic.'[18] Thus, 'art, music and poetry … are wholly taken up with practical life.'[19] The specific characteristics of poetic and religious experience are peripheral to Oakeshott's main concern with the explication of the presuppositions that underlie the world of conduct. Yet it is the passage just cited, that 'art, music and poetry are wholly taken up with practical life', which is the sentence that provoked his about-face of thirty years later in *Rationalism in Politics*. One possible reason for the forthright character of Oakeshott's retraction in *Rationalism in Politics* may be that his brief dispatch of poetry in *Experience and Its Modes* turns out to be quite ill thought through.

Oakeshott supported his inclusion of poetic experience in the world of conduct citing a passage from the *Collected Works* of Rainer Maria Rilke. However, the passage undercuts the very conclusion that he sought to hang on it! Rilke's supposed vindication of Oakeshott's view of art is included by way of a footnote attached to his claim that 'art, music and poetry are wholly taken up with practical life'. The supporting footnote goes on to state that:

> This may appear a hard saying; but it would be going out of my way to attempt to amplify it here. Instead, I will put this passage from Rilke. 'Art is childhood. Art means not to know that the world already exists, and to make a world: not

---

[18]   *Experience and Its Modes*, p. 296.

[19]   *Ibid.*, p. 297.

destroying what is found already existing, but simply not finding anything ready to hand. Nothing but possibilities and wishes ... A song, a picture which you treasure, a poem which you love, all this has its value and significance. I mean for him who creates it for the first time, and for him who creates it for the second time; for the artist and for him who really appreciates.'[20]

Oakeshott's inclusion of the passage from Rilke is understandable in supporting his view of poetic experience as expressing a sensibility rather than some external accoutrement. It goes quite against his philosophical statement, however, that art is wholly taken up with the world of conduct.

Rilke's depiction of artistic appreciation has no place in the world of conduct (at least as Oakeshott understood it). It will be remembered that Oakeshott argued that the world of conduct suffers from abstraction, because it presupposes experience to consist of, not a single world, but two ultimately incommensurable worlds: a world of 'what is' and a world of 'what ought to be'. This presupposition gives conduct its distinctive character. Now, if with this in mind, we turn to consider the passage from Rilke we find a world of experience that has no conception of 'what is'; 'art means not to know that the world already exists'. Expressed in another way, an artist's world consists only of 'what ought to be' – there is no preceding world of 'what is'.

If the little-known essay on Shylock is excluded, *Experience and Its Modes* contains Oakeshott's most forthright published declaration on the character of poetry before the publication of 'The Voice of Poetry' and his outspokenness on this occasion is unfortunate in being quite incoherent. Despite Oakeshott's confused and dismissive mention of art in *Experience and Its Modes*, it is significant because it marks the beginnings of a tension between two views of the character of poetry in his work

---

[20]   *Ibid.*, p. 297.

that are rarely distinguished one from another. On the one hand, we have his bald assertion that art is wholly taken up with conduct in life. On the other, we find him attempting to support this claim with a passage which, at least at first glance, runs at odds to his conclusion and distinguishes poetry from the world of conduct. From the 1930s onwards the project of identifying the place of poetry within the social whole and thus specifying the character of poetry in its own terms occupies an increasingly prominent place in Oakeshott's work.

Finally, the idea of poetic experience as referring to the moral sensibilities of a self rather than moral achievement in terms of an external order of things is not confined to Oakeshott's early writings. Intimations of poetic experience as sensibility and its affinity with religious experience can be detected in the passage in which Oakeshott explored self-enactment as religious experience in *On Human Conduct*. Oakeshott described an 'enacted self [as] itself a fugitive; not a generic unity but a dramatic identity without benefit of a model of self-perfection.'[21] I cite the passage only to make the point that understanding poetic experience as sensibility is not simply a stage that the 'young Oakeshott' went through. Poetic experience remained for Oakeshott, at least in one of his moods, a condition which described a heightened attention of a self to its interior order.

2. Poetry as an Autonomous World of Experience

In a number of works that were composed and published in the three decades after *Experience and Its Modes*, Oakeshott began to explore the character of poetic experience in its own terms rather than as an exemplification of religious and moral experience. The next significant point in the development of

---

[21]   *On Human Conduct*, p. 84.

his conception of the character of poetry occurred in 1938. This year is significant, not for anything that Oakeshott published, but because of the appearance of two books that exerted a noticeable influence over his view of the character of art. The works are Collingwood's *The Principles of Art* and Johan Huizinga's *Homo Ludens*.[22] Oakeshott reviewed the former of these works in the year that it appeared and he referred to the latter in a number of works after it first appeared in English in 1949.[23]

The Principles of Art and *Homo Ludens* both outline conceptions of art as play, an idea which Oakeshott expounded at length in a posthumously published and undated essay entitled 'Work and Play'.[24] 'Work' and 'play' denote distinct types of activity. On the one hand, 'work' refers to activity that 'aims to change the world, to use it, to make something out of it ... to exert power over the hostile world, to subdue it, and to extract from it what may be useful in satisfying wants ... [it] is to impress some temporary human purpose upon some compo-

---

[22]   R.G. Collingwood, *The Principles of Art*, (Oxford, Clarendon Press, 1938) and J. Huizinga, *Homo Ludens: proeve leuer bepeking van het spel-element der cultuur*, (Haarlem, H.D. Tjeenk Willink, 1938). *Homo Ludens* first appeared in English as *Homo Ludens: A Study of the Play-Element in Culture*, (London, Routledge, 1949).

[23]   See *Cambridge Review* 59, (1937–8), p. 487.

[24]   Luke O'Sullivan dates 'Work and Play' as 'c.1960', which locates its composition after 'The Voice of Poetry'. See M. Oakeshott, *What is History and Other Essays: Selected Writings Vol. 1*, (ed. L. O'Sullivan, Imprint Academic, 2004). A case could be made for this essay having been composed in the late 1940s or early 1950s. Firstly *Homo Ludens* was published in English in 1949 and it may not have been available to Oakeshott before or during the war. The influence of *Homo Ludens* on Oakeshott is reflected in his discussion of the politics of scepticism as play in *The Politics of Faith and the Politics of Scepticism*, the composition of which Fuller dates around 1952, and he also refers to Huizinga in 'The Activity of Being an Historian' and *The Harvard Lectures*, each of which was published and delivered in 1958.

nent of the world.'[25] On the other hand, 'play' characterises activity in which the aim is 'to illuminate the world, to see it as it is … to discern the intelligibility of the world … '[26] Poetry, like philosophy, science and history is a playful activity which is distinct from the mundane world of work. Poetry is, further-more, 'even more securely insulated from any liability of being confused with the satisfaction of wants than these explanatory activities. It is also less likely to be corrupted by it.'[27] In 'Work and Play', Oakeshott not only rejected the reduction of poetry to an idiom of the world of conduct, but he distinguished poetry above all other types of playful activity from the activity of work. 'Work and Play' displays clearly Oakeshott's rejection of the type of reduction of poetic experience to an idiom of conduct that he asserted in *Experience and Its Modes*. This essay marks a sea change in Oakeshott's characterisation of poetry. In his works up to and including *Experience and Its Modes*, the character of poetry is significant primarily as an exemplar of religious experience. In 'Work and Play', how-ever, the character of poetry is no longer exemplary but has become of interest in itself.

If we return to consider Oakeshott's review of Colling-wood's *Principles of Art*, we find an intimation of the argument of 'Work and Play', when he described the subject of his review as 'the work of an artist and a philosopher.'[28] In 'The Claims of Politics', published in the year after this review, Oakeshott continued to associate the artist with the philoso-pher. He described 'the genius of the poet and the artist and to a lesser extent of the philosopher is to create and recreate the

[25]   M. Oakeshott, 'Work and Play', (Original typescript), p. 13.

[26]   *Ibid.*

[27]   *Ibid.*, p. 14.

[28]   *Cambridge Review*, 59 (1937–8), p. 487.

values of their society.'[29] Oakeshott's association of art and philosophy in terms of their excluding political considerations forms the basis of W. H. Greenleaf's observation that 'only a few years [after *Experience and Its Modes*, Oakeshott] appears to have second thoughts about his view of aesthetic experience.'[30] Greenleaf's view is confirmed on Oakeshott's return to academic pursuits after World War Two, when his interest came to be focused, for a time, upon Hobbes's *Leviathan*. In 1947 he composed a radio broadcast entitled 'The "Collective Dream of Civilization"' and re-published later as '*Leviathan*: a Myth', in which *Leviathan* is treated as a work of 'literature in the proper sense'.[31] This essay, more than any other of Oakeshott's works, details the character of poetry as the creation of value alluded to in 'The Claims of Politics'.

Before proceeding to recount Oakeshott's characterisation of *Leviathan* as a work of literature in the proper sense, his approach in this essay should clearly be distinguished from his more famous introduction to *Leviathan*, published in the preceding year.[32] In his introduction to *Leviathan* Oakeshott proclaimed his subject as 'the greatest, perhaps the sole masterpiece of political philosophy in the English language.'[33] Oakeshott's unabashed praise of *Leviathan* as a masterpiece of political philosophy is not merely an expression of admiration at Hobbes's philosophical excellence. He was also indicating how he thought this work may most profitably be read: 'the context of the masterpiece, the setting in which its meaning is revealed, can in the nature of things be nothing narrower than

---

[29] *Religion, Politics and the Moral Life*, p. 95.

[30] Greenleaf, *Oakeshott's Philosophical Politics*, p. 30.

[31] M. Oakeshott, *Listener*, 37 (1947). Republished in 1975 as 'Leviathan: *A Myth*' in *Hobbes on Civil Association*.

[32] Hobbes, *Leviathan*. Republished in *Hobbes on Civil Association* and the Fuller edition of *Rationalism in Politics*.

[33] *Rationalism in Politics*, p. 223.

the history of political philosophy.'[34] Oakeshott understood *Leviathan* in a context of other masterpieces of political philosophy, among these, Plato's *Republic*, Augustine's *City of God* and Hegel's *Philosophy of Right*.[35]

In '*Leviathan*: a Myth' Oakeshott ignored the approach that he set out in his best known contribution to Hobbes scholarship, declaring instead that '*Leviathan* has passed for a book of philosophy and a book about politics ... But I believe it to be a work of art in the proper sense, one of the masterpieces of the literature of our language and civilization.'[36] Once again, Oakeshott's praise for *Leviathan*, this time as a literary masterpiece, entails a particular manner of reflecting upon this work. *Leviathan* 'is no longer lost to all except a few professionals, who (as like as not) understand it only professionally.'[37] Appreciated as a poetic image, *Leviathan* requires no professional knowledge of a canonical tradition of the masterpieces in western political philosophy, all that is required is a reader who is disposed to contemplate and delight in its imagery.

Regarded poetically, then, *Leviathan* is not a theoretical account or explanation of the conditions of human association. Debate concerning whether Hobbes's sovereign is constituted primarily in the amoral terms of interest, desire and power, or in the moral terms of authority and right, and the necessity of God in all of this, are to one side of the poetic qualities of *Leviathan*.[38] *Leviathan* is, rather, an image of, and an image within, a

---

[34]   *Ibid.*

[35]   *Ibid.*, pp. 225–8.

[36]   *Hobbes on Civil Association*, p. 150.

[37]   *Ibid.*

[38]   The debate between Skinner and Warrender shows what this sort of engagement looks like. See, for example, Q. Skinner, 'The Ideological Context of Hobbes's Political Thought', *The Historical Journal*, 9 (1969), 'Conquest and Consent: Thomas Hobbes and the Engagement Controversy' in *The Interregnum: The Quest for Settlement 1646–1660*, (ed. G.E. Aylmer) (London, Macmillan, 1972), 'Warrender and Skinner on

collective dream: '"In so far as the soul is in the body", says Plotinus, "it lies in deep sleep." What a people dreams in this earthly sleep is its civilization. And the substance of this dream is a myth, an imaginative interpretation of human existence, the perception (not the solution) of the mystery of human life.'[39] Every member of a civilisation belongs to their civilisation in so far as they participate in its collective dream.

The manner of participation varies widely and, in terms of the dream, different modes of participation express different levels of freedom or power. For the most part, 'We whose participation in the dream is imperfect and largely passive are, in a sense, its slaves.'[40] Passive participation in the dream through the day-to-day living of one's life, going through the motions as it were, involves merely receiving the dream. In this state, it is as if life happens to a person – a life lived mundanely without appreciation or awe. There are, however, also other types of participation in the dream, for instance, 'the scientist, whose perverse genius it is to dream that he is awake.'[41] The explanatory endeavours of science attempt 'to solve the mystery, to wake us from our dream, to destroy the myth; and were this project fully achieved, not only should we find ourselves awake in a profound darkness, but a dreadful insomnia would settle upon mankind, not less intolerable for being only a nightmare.'[42] The scientist seeks after truth but, in terms of the dream, this search may easily take on the air of an icono-

---

Hobbes: A Reply', *Political Studies*, 36 (1979), H. Warrender, *The Political Philosophy of Thomas Hobbes: His Theory of Obligation*, (Oxford, Clarendon Press, 1957) and 'Political Theory and Historiography: A Reply to Professor Skinner', *The Historical Journal*, 22 (1979).

[39]   *Hobbes on Civil Association*, p. 150.

[40]   *Ibid.*, pp. 150–1.

[41]   *Ibid.*, p. 151.

[42]   *Ibid.*, p. 151. Cf. Oakeshott's rendition of Plato's allegory of the cave in *On Human Conduct*, pp. 27–31.

clasm, the point of which is to destroy the dream.[43] The search for truth, represented in this instance by scientific endeavour, opposes the 'illusion' of the dream with a waking 'reality'. It finds merit in breaking the dream with the light of 'truth'.

Poetry and literature suppose no distinction between reality and the dream. This is not to say that, in poetry, reality is mistaken for the dream or the dream for reality (poetic images are not illusions), but that this opposition simply does not exist:

> The office of literature in a civilization is not to break the dream but to recall it and even to make more articulate the dream-powers of a people ... the comparative freedom of the artist springs not from any faculty of wakefulness (not from any opposition to the dream), but from his power to dream more profoundly; his genius is to dream that he is dreaming ... The gift of the greatest literature – of poetry – is a gift of imagination. Its effect is an expansion of our faculty of dreaming. Under its inspiration the familiar outlines of the common dream fade, new perceptions, and emotions hitherto unfelt, are excited within us, the till-now settled fact dissolves once more into infinite possibility, and we become aware that the myth (which is the substance of the dream) has acquired a new quality, without our needing to detect the precise character of the change.[44]

Oakeshott's description of poetic genius as the dreaming of the collective dream elaborates upon his account of poetic

[43] The presentation of science as an iconoclasm may recall Nietzsche's *Twilight of the Idols: Or How One Philosophizes with a Hammer*, such a reading would, however, miss the subtlety in Nietzsche's title. As Kaufmann points out in his 'Editor's Preface', Nietzsche had originally entitled the work *A Psychologist's Idleness* and changed the title as 'an afterthought'. See *The Portable Nietzsche*, (ed. W. Kaufmann) (Harmondsworth, Penguin, 1984), pp. 463–4. Kaufmann points out that 'It is usually assumed that [Nietzsche] means a sledge hammer. The preface, however, from which the title is derived ... explains: "idols are here touched as with a tuning fork."' When read in context the poetry in Nietzsche's image is unmistakable: 'The essay ... is above all a recreation, a spot of sunshine, a leap sideways into the idleness of a psychologist.', p. 466.

[44] *Hobbes on Civil Association*, pp. 150–1.

activity as the creation and recreation of the values of society and distinguishes this type of activity from both the explanatory worlds of theoretical experience and the mundane world of conduct. I shall explore the detail of Oakeshott's rendition of the poetic qualities of *Leviathan* in the next section.

In '*Leviathan*: A Myth', Oakeshott provided his most detailed account of the distinctively creative character of poetic imagining. All that remains to complete his philosophical account of poetry is the explication of the distinctive presuppositions underlying poetic experience that he undertook in 'The Voice of Poetry in the Conversation of Mankind'. Oakeshott's review of Collingwood's *Principles of Art*, the publication of 'The Claims of Politics' and '*Leviathan*: A Myth' and the composition of 'Work and Play', are, philosophically understood, mere preludes to 'The Voice of Poetry'. In 'The Voice of Poetry', Oakeshott argued that the character of poetic experience is autonomous from other types of experience, because it presupposes experience as supposition rather than judgement. Poetic images imply no truth claim and thus they do not distinguish between 'fact' and 'not fact'. Poetic experience constitutes an escape from the world of conduct as well as the explanatory worlds of science, history and philosophy.

The influence of Collingwood's *Speculum Mentis* looms large in Oakeshott's distinction of the character of poetry from the more familiar voices of conduct and science at the beginning of 'The Voice of Poetry'.[45] Collingwood distinguished artistic, religious and scientific forms of experience from one another in terms of a distinctive relation between symbol (language) and meaning (thought) operating throughout each world of experience. In the world of conduct a symbol and its meaning are distinct from one another, but meaning is not radically separable from its symbol; as Oakeshott put it, 'every word [as far as is possible] has its proper reference or significa-

---

[45] 'The Voice of Poetry', Sects. 3 and 4.

tion.'[46] This characteristic is perhaps most pronounced in religion that, for Collingwood as well as Oakeshott, is the apogee of life. A religious symbol points beyond itself to a meaning, as when the relics of a martyr are valued not for what they are, shards of bone, but for what they mean — the faith to sacrifice one's all for God and the faith in this action of those who attend the relic.[47] The relic means more than it is, but it is a symbol which is not freely exchangeable with other symbols. It is important that the sacred object is, in fact, water from the grotto at Lourdes and not common rain water.[48] And thus, in the world of conduct 'we do not seek to enlarge the meanings [of signs] … speaking here is expressing or conveying images and is not itself image-making.'[49]

Science is distinct from the world of conduct and religion in reversing the precedence of symbol and meaning. Collingwood argued that while in religion language (symbol) exerts a tyranny over thought (meaning), in science '[l]anguage falls into its place as the mere servant of thought, and science treats it despotically, making it mean just what it likes … '[50] In science, symbol and meaning are not only distinct from one another as they are in religion, meaning is liberated from symbol. In liberating meaning from symbol, science is 'more precisely symbolic [than conduct]: when [words in scientific utterance] can be refined no further, they give place not to gestures, but to technical expression and mathematical symbols

---

[46] *Rationalism in Politics*, p. 504.

[47] Collingwood, *Speculum Mentis*, pp. 126–8.

[48] Collingwood went on to argue that this is why religious wars have been amongst the most vicious of conflicts. He believed that persecution is an integral component of religious experience because of the inseparability of symbol and meaning. Religious factions do not generally respect the religiosity of other factions but find other forms of devotion blasphemous. See *Speculum Mentis*, pp. 116–7.

[49] *Rationalism in Politics*, p. 503.

[50] Collingwood, *Speculum Mentis*, p. 157.

... '[51] In scientific discourse a symbol is both distinguishable and separable from the meaning that it conveys. For instance, the area of a circle divided by its radius squared equals π. As a scientific or mathematical *symbol*, 'π' is inconsequential. The meaning of 'π' may be symbolised just as satisfactorily by the notation area/radius squared, or 22/7, and less accurately (and so less scientifically) as 3.14. In all (perhaps bar the last) of these denotations, meaning is the primary consideration. At any rate, the worlds of conduct and scientific experience consist, in varying degrees, of symbolic discourse that distinguish symbol from meaning and in which symbol is a means of conveying meaning.

Oakeshott also followed Collingwood in arguing that poetic experience is distinct from the worlds of scientific and religious experience in being non-symbolic:

> in the language of poetry, words, shapes, sounds, movements are not signs with preordained significances ... they are not 'conveyances' when what is to be conveyed exists already in thought or emotion ... In poetry words are themselves images and not signs for other images ... [52]

In poetic imagining symbol and meaning are not only inseparable as they are in practical language, in poetry they are indistinguishable. A poetic image is its meaning; it symbolises nothing outside of itself. Van Gogh's 'Starry Night' is most certainly a poor reproduction of the heavens; practically, for purposes of navigation for instance, it is useless, and scientifically it is inaccurate beyond belief. However, van Gogh was not concerned to produce a useful piece of information or an accurate representation of the night sky. Viewed as a poetic image, 'Starry Night' is not even an attempt to convey an emotion; it is

---

[51]   *Rationalism in Politics*, p. 508.
[52]   *Ibid.*, p. 527, cf Collingwood,. *Speculum Mentis*, Ch. 4, Sect. 4.

simply an image to be contemplated and delighted in.[53] There is no reference, no starry night, outside of the frame of van Gogh's image.

Oakeshott did not deny that poetic images may become practical images and *vice versa*. However, he maintained that a poetic image regarded (or used) for practical purposes is no longer a poetic image. The use, for example, of 'art' for instruction is religion or propaganda and, in its most 'brutal and vulgar' form, 'art' as amusement is pornography; and propaganda and pornography are not bad art, they are simply not art at all.[54] This is not to say that artistic images cannot become religious symbols, edifying parables or even be used as amusements. A moral tale can be found in Milton's *Paradise Lost* – pride comes before a fall – and the theological disputes of the day explain his extended treatment of some otherwise curious asides.[55] These considerations may be valid moral and historical concerns. The images that populate the pages of *Paradise Lost* may also be regarded as images in which to delight – Satan lately landed in Hell 'round throws his baleful eyes' or the advent of Raphael in Paradise

> Like Maia's son he stood
> And shook his plumes, that heav'nly fragrance filled
> The circuit wide.[56]

---

[53] See *Rationalism in Politics*, p. 526, 'quite clearly, [Keats' Ode to Melancholy] could have been composed by a man of sanguine temperament who never himself felt the touch of melancholy; clearly, also, it is not designed to excite melancholy in the reader (or, if that were its design, it fails signally); and it cannot be said to tell us what melancholy really is.'

[54] See Collingwood, *Principles of Art*, pp. 84–5.

[55] For example, the description of the feast set by Eve for Raphael is, beside being an image of plenitude in Paradise, an affirmation of Milton's belief that angels are corporeal beings. See *Paradise Lost*, Bk. 5, Lines 397–467, pp. 308–9.

[56] *Paradise Lost*, Bk. 1, Line 56, p. 213 and Bk. 5, Lines 285–8, p. 305.

These images are indistinguishable from what they mean. Different phrasing would constitute different images; in poetry one may not substitute 'sunlit field of grass' for 'golden meadow'.[57] Regarded poetically, there is nothing signified by Milton's Satan outside of the dramatic appreciation of the character itself. A poetic image is no more or less than the symbols in which its author has created it.

Aestheticians alive to the history of their discipline and the relatively recent advent of the modern, non-representational theory of art propounded by Oakeshott may be ready with objections. It could be argued that Oakeshott's non-symbolic account of art has next to no commerce before Kant and the 'expressivism' of the Romantics, and thus that 'true' poetic experience is restricted to only an extremely narrow sector of humanity – namely late modern European civilisation. The classical and medieval periods in Europe (not to mention the rest of the world) are, on this understanding, largely devoid of poetic experience.[58] Such a view would suffer an ethnocentrism that Oakeshott's historical understanding of human activity is at pains to avoid. He did indeed take issue with the Platonic account of art as technical imitation and it could also reasonably be argued that medieval religious art had more to do with religious than poetic experience concerned, as it so often was, with instruction on the damnation and salvation of

---

[57]   *Rationalism in Politics.* p. 528, also p. 525, 'The changes poets are apt to make in their work are not strictly speaking, 'correction' – that is to say, attempts to improve the 'expression' of an already clear mental image; they are attempts to imagine more clearly and to delight more deeply.'

[58]   Although Oakeshott offers a qualification: 'Of the East I hesitate to speak. But there is a significant anecdote of Chuang Tzu about Ch'ing, the chief carpenter of the Prince of Lu, whose description of the activity of being an artist is almost entirely in terms of what he had to forget [ie. his practical experience].' *Rationalism in Politics*, p. 531.

souls.[59] But Oakeshott's view does not forbid him from observing that 'there have always been poets, and there have always been "works of art" in the sense in which I have used the expression, I see no reason to doubt; but the activity of the persons has not always been acknowledged and the character of the images as poetic images has often been obscured.'[60] So, all that Oakeshott is actually claiming is that some situations may be more or less conducive to expressing or recognising a poetic sensibility than others. Some circumstances conspire against the recognition of a poetic sensibility as, for instance, when art is subject to religious categories such as blasphemy.[61] Poetic insight, if it is not being actively disavowed, is, more often than not, ignored by its contemporary culture.[62]

A final re-affirmation of Oakeshott's argument for the autonomous character of poetic experience occurs in *On Human Conduct* in his brief distinction between poetic activity

---

[59] In 'The Voice of Poetry' Oakeshott is perhaps overly disparaging of Plato's theory of art, *Rationalism in Politics*, pp. 511–2. For a more generous treatment of Plato's theory of art see Collingwood's *Principles of Art*, Bk. 1, Ch. 2, Sect. 2 and Ch. 5, Sect. 5. Oakeshott endorses Huizinga's view of medieval conceptions of art in *The Harvard Lectures*, p. 6: 'It has been noted by Huizinga that the Middle Ages knew only what may be called applied art. The artist was recognized, and recognized himself, as a man who adorned, decorated and illustrated the activities that were afoot in a medieval community; his work was not desired and valued for its own sake but for the contribution it made to current ways of living.'

[60] *Rationalism in Politics*, p. 530.

[61] There are parallels between the emergence of art as an autonomous world of experience and the emergence of science; consider, for instance, the interest of the Roman Church in Galileo's astronomy. Cf. Collingwood, *Speculum Mentis*, pp. 30–5.

[62] See Collingwood *Speculum Mentis*, p. 18, 'Ours, we say, is an age of little men: how can we care for their work? . . . . Send us another Keats, and we will listen. Good sirs, if the soul of Keats could be re-embodied upon earth, you would treat him as your fathers treated him before. You have learned by now to like his Odes; but if he came to earth again he would not repeat them, but write something as far in advance of this age as his Odes were in advance of that.'

and conduct. He identified conduct and poetic appreciation as the idiomatically distinct activities of 'acting' and 'fabricating';

> In 'acting' the imagined and wished-for outcomes of the agent's performances is the response looked for in the performances of other agents or in himself when he comes (as he must) to respond to what he has done; and every such performance is an episode in an interminable adventure. In 'fabricating' the imagined and wished-for outcome is an artefact; a finished product.[63]

Oakeshott made it clear that his engagement to theorise human conduct does not 'exclude fabrication, but only … what is unique to fabrication, namely a work of art properly so called.'[64] He acknowledged that fabricating, making artefacts, may constitute a type of conduct *inter homines* 'where artefacts are produced for sale, in building a bridge or a ship … ' and so on.[65] However, fabricating, when it involves making 'works of art in the proper sense', is not conduct *inter homines* and so falls outside the field of his present concerns. An artefact regarded as an end in itself rather than as an instrument for on-going conduct *inter homines* remains within the bounds of poetic experience.

Thus far the development of Oakeshott's account of poetic experience has been set out as consisting of three stages. First, Oakeshott included poetry within the world of conduct. This is the position of *Experience and Its Modes* and it is confirmed as consisting of more than a single foolish sentence in a number of references to the character of poetry in earlier essays. Second, in works after *Experience and Its Modes* Oakeshott began, at least implicitly, to distinguish the character of poetry from other types of experience. This position was developed through book reviews and published and unpublished essays

---

[63] *On Human Conduct*, p. 35.

[64] *Ibid.*, p. 36.

[65] *Ibid.*, p. 35.

composed from the late 1930s through to the 1950s. Finally, Oakeshott demonstrated the explicit philosophical grounds of his distinction between poetry and other worlds of experience in 'The Voice of Poetry'. This view of the steady development of Oakeshott's characterisation of poetry supports Greenleaf's account of Oakeshott's aesthetic. If Oakeshott's characterisation of poetic experience changed radically from *Experience and Its Modes* to 'The Voice of Poetry', it is at least a change in a single direction. On the above account, Grant's observation, with which I began the chapter, that 'For Oakeshott, in the end, Poetry remains ambiguous, paradoxical and plural', appears overly harsh.[66] A change in a single direction, no matter how radical, need not be ambiguous, paradoxical or plural. In fact, if anything, it can be argued that Oakeshott became more unequivocal, clear and singular in his view of the character of poetic experience.

3. Poetic Experience and the Collective Dream

The three-stage progression of the development of Oakeshott's account of the character of poetry appears to counter Grant's attribution of lack of clarity in this matter. The development of Oakeshott's characterisation of poetic experience as an autonomous world is not, however, the only level on which he explored poetry. Oakeshott's work on poetry is not confined to understanding poetic experience in terms of the presuppositions it makes about the character of reality, it is also manifest in his account of what he referred to as 'philosophical literature'.[67] In philosophical literature the demonstrative and definitive philosophical character of Oakeshott's aesthetics gives way to a more conversational, expansive and

---

[66] Grant, *Oakeshott*, p. 109.

[67] *Hobbes on Civil Association*, p. 150. Oakeshott also tried his hand at poetry, see 'Scutari' and 'Cracow', *Cambridge Review*, 53 (1931-2).

evocative language.[68] Oakeshott's usually rigorous categorial demarcations between worlds of experience are (often frustratingly) absent and he is found writing, rather, in the fashion of a literary critic who 'quickens the hearing we give to the voice of poetry and explores the qualities of the poem'. [69] In philosophical literature Oakeshott explored poetic images, not in terms of them constituting an autonomous world of experience, but rather in their own poetic terms as constituting a vision of what we have come to know ourselves to be.

Attending to Oakeshott's account of philosophical literature provides grounds for re-considering the significance of his characterisations of poetic experience in works after *Experience and Its Modes*. His reference to poetry as the creation and recreation of value in 'The Claims of Politics', for instance, takes on a considerably altered significance to that presented by Greenleaf. It will be remembered that Greenleaf interpreted Oakeshott's assertion that 'the genius of the poet and the artist and to a lesser extent of the philosopher is to create and recreate the values of their society' as signalling Oakeshott's second thoughts about the reduction of poetry to an idiom within the world of conduct. While Oakeshott's association of the poet and the writer with the philosopher may intimate his later philosophical arguments for the autonomy of poetry, his affirmation of poetic activity as the creation and recreation of the values of society presents a far more ambiguous picture of the relation between poetry and the world of conduct.[70]

Oakeshott's description of poetic activity as the creation and recreation of values conveys moral (and religious) overtones that are reminiscent of thinkers such as Yeats, Rilke and Nietz-

---

[68]   G. Johnson described the language of 'The Voice of Poetry' as 'heavily philosophical', *Poetry Review*, 51 (1960), p. 43.

[69]   *Rationalism in Politics*, p. 495.

[70]   In contrast to Greenleaf, Grant argues that in 'The Claims of Politics' 'Oakeshott wrote in a similar vein' to *Experience and Its Modes*, Grant, *Oakeshott*, p. 104.

sche.[71] The poetic activity of creating and recreating values may escape a mundane level of work in the world of conduct (in the 'The Claims of Politics' represented by politics), without denying Oakeshott's earlier view of poetry as sharing many of the characteristics of moral and religious experience. In this essay the negative and defensive character of politics is distinguished, not only from other worlds of play, but from playful idioms within the world of conduct such as morality and religion and poetry.

The complex character of the relation between poetic experience and conduct is exemplified in Oakeshott's presentation of two myths in terms of which we have come to understand ourselves. An early modern statement of the first can be found in Oakeshott's consideration of Hobbes's *Leviathan* as a work of art in the proper sense. He framed his interpretation of *Leviathan* in terms of the myth of original sin. The myth of original sin supposes that:

> The human race, and the world it inhabits … is the creative act of God and was as perfect as its creator. But by an original sin, mankind became separated from the source of its happiness and peace. This sin was Pride, the perverse exaltation of the creature, by which man became a god unto himself … But while corrupted man pursued his blind desires, an enemy of himself and his kind, divine grace set a limit to human self-destruction, and promised a restoration of the shattered order, an ultimate salvation.[72]

Some passages of this myth resemble myths from non-Christian civilisations, 'the hubris of Homeric Greece [is, for instance,] hardly distinguishable [from] Augustinian

---

[71] See E. Heller, *The Importance of Nietzsche: Ten Essays*, (Chicago, University of Chicago Press, 1988), especially Essay 6, 'Rilke and Nietzsche with a Discourse on Thought, Belief and Poetry', and Essay 7, 'Yeats and Nietzsche: Reflections on Aestheticism and a Poet's Marginal Notes'.

[72] *Hobbes on Civil Association*, pp. 151–2.

superbia.'[73] Also, within the Christian imagination, the myth of humanity's Fall and Redemption has been imagined and re-imagined with varying degrees of profundity: 'it owes most to the imagination of St. Paul and St. Augustine'.[74] A less penetrating version (or perversion) of the myth may be found in the heresy of Pelagius.[75]

Oakeshott held that Hobbes's *Leviathan* is one of the most profound modern expressions of the Pauline and Augustinian versions of the myth.[76] Hobbes's representation of the myth of original sin is set in a post-lapsarian world after God's creation has wilfully forsaken the perfection of its original state. The divine artifice of the natural order is fallen and the children of pride are thrown upon their own finite powers of artifice.[77] In this post-lapsarian state each individual 'is solitary in the sense that he belongs to no order and has no obligations.'[78] There is no natural communion between an individual and his or her fellows and neither can these solitary creatures communicate with their Creator. As fallen creatures, however, Hobbesian individuals remain recognisably the creatures made in the image of their creator in that they create. Human

---

[73] *On Human Conduct*, p. 83.

[74] *Ibid.*, p. 152.

[75] See R.G. Collingwood and J.N.L. Meyers, *Roman Britain and the English Settlements*, 2nd edition (Oxford, Clarendon Press, 1937), p. 309, 'Pelagius in opposing [Augustine's determinism] was expressing the same paralysis of will that his countrymen were revealing in action: Augustine's thought, still to-day dominating civilization like a colossus, expressed the demonic energy of the early Christian mind, conscious of itself as drawing on stores of energy that were not finite, like the human personality, but infinite.'

[76] Perhaps Bacon's *New Atlantis* and the eschatology underlying the writings of the early Marx are the modern echoes of the Pelagian version of the myth of original sin.

[77] For Hobbes's distinction between human and divine artifice see *Rationalism in Politics*, pp. 246–7.

[78] *Hobbes on Civil Association*, p. 152.

beings are the creators of their worlds.[79] Although each individual is surrounded by a multitude of other individuals, each
is isolated from the others in dwelling in a world primarily of
his or her own making (imagination). Each individual:

> inhabits a world which contains the materials for the satisfac-
> tions of all his desires save one – the desire to continue for ever
> the enjoyment of an endless series of satisfactions … it is not
> the transitoriness of his satisfaction that hinders a man's hap-
> piness, but the constant fear that death may supervene and
> put an end to satisfaction by terminating desire. There is
> indeed a lesser fear, the fear that his natural powers will be
> insufficient to assure him of the satisfaction of his next
> desire.[80]

As often as not, the object of desire or approbation in the
world of one individual is the object of aversion or disapprobation in the worlds of other individuals and these disagree-
ments, in the absence of mediation (divine or otherwise) may
easily — will inevitably — develop into full scale conflict.
Even when an object is deemed desirable by more than one
individual, far from introducing the grounds of concord, this
object gives rise to competition. Thus a multitude of solitary
individuals constitutes a war of all against all, and this calami-
tous condition is the emblem of the finitude of humanity in its
lapsed condition. The war of all against all is a condition in
which the likelihood of the greatest evil, a violent death, is
foremost in one's mind and in which, even if one manages to
avoid this fate, survival and mere existence occupy one's

---

[79]   See R.E. Flathman, *Thomas Hobbes: Skepticism, Individuality and Chastened
       Politics*, (Newbury Park, Sage, 1993), p. 1, 'Thomas Hobbes is first and
       foremost a theorist of individual human beings as the *Makers* of them-
       selves and their worlds.'

[80]   *Hobbes on Civil Association*, p. 152.

imaginative powers almost entirely.[81] The finite powers of human imagination are not only powerful enough to corrupt the divinely inspired natural order, however, they are also capable of delivering humanity, at least in part, from the devastating consequences of its fall from grace. The lesser fear of insufficient power to secure the satisfaction of one's next desire 'may be ignored by those who possess a certain nobility of temperament which refuses the indignity of unconditional competition, or it may be removed by coming to some agreement with his fellow inhabitants of the world, an agreement which may establish a kind of superficial peace and orderliness. But the great fear, the fear of death is permanent and unassuaged.'[82] Neither does the poetic quality of *Leviathan* lie in any practical solution it may offer in dealing with the trials and tribulations of life.

Hobbes painted his image of fallen humanity upon a canvas of Brueghelesque proportions. His world is filled with creatures undertaking a diverse range of activities in which they create and occupy their individual worlds of finite delight and finite sorrow and in doing so perhaps escape, for a time, the greater fear of the cessation of imagining in death. Oakeshott concluded his account of *Leviathan* in the style of the literary critic, observing that 'To those brought up in the older myth, [*Leviathan*] will appear an unduly disenchanted interpretation of the mystery of human life ... Certainly it appeared shocking

---

[81]   Thus Hobbes's famous description of a state of nature: 'In such a condition there is no place for industry; because the fruit thereof is uncertain: and consequently no cultivation of the earth; no navigation, nor use of the commodities that may be imported by sea; no commodious building; no instruments of moving, and removing, such things as require much force; no knowledge of the face of the earth; no account of time; no arts; no letters; no society; and which is worst of all, continual fear, and danger of violent death; and the life of man, solitary, poor, nasty, brutish and short.' *Leviathan*, Ch. 13, Sect. 5, p. 82.

[82]   *Hobbes on Civil Association*, pp. 152–3.

to Hobbes's contemporaries … '[83] Hobbes did not imagine an idealised past in which a divinely sanctioned natural order prevailed in human affairs and to which, if we could not return, we might at least approach or cease to move away from — the inspiration underlying Filmer's *Patriarchia,* as well as Locke's *Second Treatise*. He did not imagine that humanity possessed the ability to save itself from its predicament, the Pelagian version of the myth that Bacon re-vitalised in his *New Atlantis*. Hobbes 'lived at the moment in our history when the potentiality of the traditional myth was ready to declare itself, but before the tide of science, with its project of destroying all myth, had begun to sweep over our civilization.'[84] The magnificence of the medieval myth of original sin had faded by Hobbes's time, but rather than deride the myth as superstition on this account, *Leviathan* recast the myth in terms which ensured that it endured as a

> passage in the common dream … that our literature since the seventeenth century has not allowed us to forget … [Hobbes] with a sure and steady irony, does what Swift could do with only an intermittent brilliance, and what the literature of Existentialism is doing today with an exaggerated display of emotion and a false suggestion of novelty.[85]

Hobbes's rendering of the myth of original sin is often derided and dismissed as the product of an overly pessimistic mind; a misanthropic blot on the optimism of the Renaissance. However, on Oakeshott's reading of Hobbes, in recognising the limitations of humanity, its creative powers are brought to light. Humanity is not entirely beyond redemption and is capable of doing something, however inadequate, that sets in place the conditions that allow individuals to explore and enjoy living the good life. Leviathan is indubitably a creature

[83]   *Ibid.*, p. 153.

[84]   *Ibid.*, p. 154.

[85]   *Ibid.*

of human making – it arises in the recognition that humans cannot save themselves. The recognition of the limited powers of humanity (which are nonetheless powers) is itself a condition of salvation. If we return to the early Christian renditions of this myth we find both Paul and Augustine conceiving of humanity as beyond redemption by its own powers – grace is by definition undeserved. But neither writer understood human incapacity as constituting an excuse to quit the quest for salvation. Both viewed the hopeless condition of humanity as calling for redoubled efforts to 'justify' oneself to God even though they acknowledged the inevitability of falling short in this venture.

The second myth in terms of which Oakeshott identified the human condition is the tower of Babel. The tower of Babel is, like *Leviathan*, a story of humanity set in a post-lapsarian world. In the case of Hobbes's *Leviathan*, the children of pride are tamed by a construction of their own making. The tower of Babel provides a version of events whereby what is constructed is emblematic of the undoing of the proud. Far from being opposed to the myth of original sin, the tower of Babel supports its insights by relating the disastrous consequences of taking upon oneself the liberation of oneself and one's fellows from the predicament of being human. The tower of Babel is well known as an emblem for the failure of any exercise by which humanity presumes that it will get into Heaven by a sheer act of will; 'In some of the stories that revolve around Nimrod ... [he] is not a petty thief ... he is the leader of a cosmic revolution whose enterprise is not only doomed to failure but entails the destruction of all the virtues and consolations of the *vitae temporalis*, a destruction of which the confusion of tongues is only emblematic.'[86]

Before concluding 'The Tower of Babel' with a rendition of the myth where the 'banalities of modernity qualify the hero-

---

[86] *On History*, p. 174.

ism of ancient impiety',[87] Oakeshott identified versions of the myth as developed by the ancient Hebrews and Greeks, Muslims, and the Caldeans.[88] He also added to his account a brief characterisation of myth (what he called stories) in the collective dream of civilisation and thus the character of the collective dream itself:

> A proper story is like a river ... what it becomes reflects the scenery through which it flows. It has a history, and its history is marked by the appearance of new incidents or new characters; its colours change; it is told in fresh idioms; it may be concentrated into a ballad or a song only to be dispersed again in more prosaic tellings.
>
> And a proper story has another quality besides this capacity to mirror the changes of human circumstances. It is the expression of some unchanging human predicament; as a Highland lament, composed to reconcile a passionate people to a contingent misfortune, expresses all the sorrows suffered by mankind since the beginning of time.[89]

The stories or myths that constitute the collective dreams of civilisations are not unique to these civilisations; they occur as variations on themes reflecting the contingent circumstances in which they are retold, as well as maintaining a version of the predicament that is the common lot of all humanity.

Each of the myths explored by Oakeshott has parallels with his accounts of the morality of the individual and the morality of the anti-individual. The myth of original sin expounded in terms of Hobbes's *Leviathan* counsels an acceptance of one's present condition and limited powers that I have identified underlying the ideas of moral salvation and the terms of moral association implied in the morality of the individual. And the tower of Babel counsels against the folly of sacrificing one's

[87] *Ibid.*, p. 176.

[88] *Ibid.*, pp. 167 and 172–3.

[89] *Ibid.*, p. 165.

present enjoyments, no matter how imperfect, for the mere (and inevitably false) promise of perfection in the future. The analogies between the leviathan and the individual, and the tower and the anti-individual, refer to the contingencies that accompany modern European conceptions of morality; but the myths can also be recognised as expressing a view of the predicament that accompanies, and may be said to constitute, life in general. Both myths observe the importance of acknowledging the limited abilities of humanity. The leviathan promises that attention to these limitations is a condition of receiving some present enjoyment in life and the tower cautions that defiance of these limits will result in certain failure and misery.

Collective dreams and the myths in terms of which they are constituted arise out of poetic reflection on the human condition. Cautions and recommendations can most certainly be drawn from these myths but this is not the business of the poet. The poet, as a contributor to the collective, reminds a society of the distinctive ways in which it has responded to the predicament that all find in conducting themselves in life. Where a society becomes bored of its way of life and takes its achievements for granted, the poet's images will not gather an audience except perhaps as amusement or for some other ulterior motive such as their investment value. In this situation a society not only takes its way of life for granted, it takes life itself for granted. And if, from the meager references to a general condition or predicament that accompanies life in Oakeshott's work, some response might be constructed that could be presented in terms of a purpose general to life, it might go along the lines of establishing the importance of living poetically. Living poetically should be taken as indicating no more than appreciating and delighting in life in a way that is not taking it for granted.

The influence of Collingwood's writings on art is, once again, readily apparent in Oakeshott's account of the role of the poet in society. Collingwood described the power of the poet in the following terms:

> As spokesman of his community, the secrets he must utter are theirs. The reason why they need him is that no community altogether knows its own heart; and by failing in this knowledge a community deceives itself on the one subject concerning which ignorance means death. For the evils which come from that ignorance the poet as prophet suggests no remedy, because he has already given one. The remedy is the poem itself. Art is the community's medicine for the worst disease of the mind, the corruption of consciousness.[90]

Oakeshott repeated these sentiments almost verbatim in a review published in the year after 'Leviathan: a myth'. He observed that 'In art, insight (diagnosis) is an end in itself. The remedy is not something that *follows*: if it is anywhere it lies in the diagnosis itself in the removal of the corrupt consciousness.'[91] Poetic images are to be contemplated and delighted in, but contemplation and delight do not denote the morally inert musings of the aesthete. Poetic images constitute an identifiably distinct idiom of utterance that is neither instruction in nor distraction from the business of living. The poetic image reminds us that we are alive and of the ways in which we have come to respond to the invitation to live both individually and collectively.

---

[90] Collingwood, *Principles of Art*, p. 336.

[91] M. Oakeshott, Review of Janko Lavrin, *Nietzsche: An Approach*, in *Cambridge Journal*, 1 (1947–8), p. 450.

Chapter 6
Conclusion

It is common to conclude a study of a thinker with a summation of their contribution to a particular tradition of thought or some of the debates that are currently afoot. As a contemporary thinker Oakeshott's contribution has been plotted most commonly in terms of current debates in political philosophy (although some commentators have placed his work in the context of a broader history of thought.) I began by observing that the secondary literature generated by Oakeshott's account of conduct has largely ignored his characterisations of religious and poetic experience and focused instead upon his account of the appropriate terms of moral association. This focus has encouraged his work to be understood as a contribution to the contemporary debate between liberalism and its critics.[1] Although commentators have disagreed on the precise location of Oakeshott's work within this debate, they have

---

[1]   Examples of interpretations of Oakeshott as, on the one hand, a conventional liberal can be found in C. Covell, *The Redefinition of Conservatism: Politics and Doctrine*, (Basingstoke, Macmillan, 1986), and, on the other, as a conservative critic of liberalism in K.E. Koerner, *Liberalism and its Critics*, (London, Croom Helm, 1985).

generally agreed that it is most appropriately referred to in terms of this framework.

In concluding I shall map some of the features of the terrain in which Oakeshott's work is usually placed and, then, consider how the map is altered by recognising the significance of his characterisations of religion and poetry. In constructing this alternative account I note a number of commentators who have noticed in Oakeshott's accounts of religious and poetic experience an existentialist theme that runs through his work. I argue, however, that there is more to the picture than an indeterminate existentialist mood or theme in some passages of Oakeshott's writing. These themes go to the heart of Oakeshott's account of moral identity and they require significant specification to avoid implying some of the more solipsistic versions of the self that have been associated with existentialism. In acknowledging the significance of Oakeshott's accounts of religious and poetic experience, together with his characterisation of the terms of moral association, we gain a fuller appreciation of his account of the good life understood in terms of the three moral categories identified by Lewis: the appropriate relations between individuals, the appropriate order of a self and an idea of a purpose that is general to life.

1. Oakeshott as a Liberal and a Critic of Liberalism

John Gray has argued 'that in his conception of civil association Oakeshott has isolated and identified the very kernel of "liberalism" ... '[2] Gray is far from alone in taking this view of Oakeshott's work:

> W.H. Greenleaf and Samuel Brittan have seen in Oakeshott's thought deep affinities with the intellectual tradition of classical liberalism; an entire paper [W.J. Coates Jr. 'Michael

---

[2]   J. Gray, *Liberalism*, (London, Routledge, 1989), p. 199.

Oakeshott as Liberal Theorist', *Canadian Journal of Political Science*, 18 (1985)] … has been devoted to interpreting Oakeshott as a liberal theorist; and both of the two recent booklength studies of Oakeshott's work [Franco's *The Political Philosophy of Michael Oakeshott* and Grant's *Oakeshott*] characterize his outlook on politics as at least akin to that of a liberal.[3]

In fact, Greenleaf, Grant and Franco (and, ultimately, Gray himself) have exhibited varying degrees of reservation in associating Oakeshott's thought with liberalism. Greenleaf observed, for instance, that Oakeshott is liberal in being:

> obviously anti-socialist and hostile to many aspects of the planned society and the welfare state. [However,] he cannot, without reservation, be called a liberal for (among other things) he has explicitly said that liberalism shows a continual tendency to pursue the abstract scheme of reform, the dream of progress and human perfectibility, and to be associated with rationalism and scientism, errors which he constantly and energetically repudiated.[4]

In like manner Grant has been less than unconditional in his presentation of Oakeshott as a liberal:

> Oakeshott's politics amount to a kind of conservative liberalism or a liberal conservatism. He has a conservative's respect for tradition, and the conservative's distrust of individuality conceived, in the abstract liberal manner, as existing prior to the nexus of social activities, relations and traditions through which alone (on this view) individuality can emerge. [But, he also] has the classical liberal's distrust of dirigiste or otherwise excessive government.[5]

---

[3]   J. Gray, *Post-Liberalism: Studies in Political Thought*, (New York, Routledge, 1993), p. 40.

[4]   Greenleaf, *Oakeshott's Philosophical Politics*, p. 81.

[5]   Grant, *Oakeshott*, p. 62. Cf. O'Sullivan, *The Problem of Political Obligation*, p. 233. O'Sullivan contraposes the 'pessimistic [sceptical], conservative liberalism' of Oakeshott with the 'optimistic, reforming liberalism of Green and Bosanquet …'

Gray qualified his presentation of Oakeshott as a liberal arguing that 'The idea of civil association, though it rightly repudiates the doctrinal liberal pretension to universal authority, at the same time has reference far beyond the cultural traditions which gave issue to it.'[6] On the above understandings, Oakeshott offered 'liberal' conclusions affirming the worth of the individual and the limited character of politics. He grounded these conclusions, however, in a conception of moral practice that has far more in common with thinkers who have been understood as either conservative or radical critics of liberalism.

Franco has provided a detailed account of the type of framework brought into play in understanding Oakeshott's 'political philosophy' in terms of the debate between liberalism and its critics. Oakeshott's political philosophy is presented as a

> restatement of liberalism [which overcomes] the antinomy of 'deontological' liberalism (as represented by, say, John Rawls, Robert Nozick, Ronald Dworkin, and Friedrich Hayek) and 'communitarianism' (as represented by Michael Sandel, Charles Taylor, Richard Rorty, and Alasdair MacIntyre, amongst others).[7]

The defining poles of Franco's antinomy consist of deontological liberalism, which posits a universally valid system of liberal values, and communitarianism, which rejects the assumption of an absolute moral order. On the one hand, deontological liberals typically argue that human beings possess a common nature or rationality from which they derive an inalienable body of moral rights that belongs to each individual. This body of rights constitutes a criterion by which the moral validity, or justness, of particular values, practices and social arrangements can be measured. On the other hand, communitarians typically reject the presumption of a univer-

---

[6]   Gray, *Liberalism*, p. 212.

[7]   Franco, *The Political Philosophy of Michael Oakeshott*, p. 230.

sal body of moral rights and obligations. They argue that the moral validity of practices, values and social arrangements is grounded in the traditions that constitute particular communities. The moral validity of values and practices derives from the culture that these values and practices constitute.

Franco argued that Oakeshott's political philosophy bridges the antinomy by answering three of the most important communitarian objections that have been raised against liberalism. First, communitarians challenge the liberal assumption of an ahistorical natural subject or human nature. Communitarians argue that human nature is itself a cultural construction.[8] Second, communitarians are dissatisfied with the approach that liberals adopt toward political philosophy. Liberals write as if political philosophy ought to justify (liberal) beliefs and values rather than understand and explain the actual practices that philosophers have before them. Communitarians argue that, on the contrary, the 'task of political philosophy is not to *justify* political institutions but to *articulate* our shared intuitions and beliefs about politics.'[9] Philosophical inquiry succeeds rather than precedes moral and political practices. Third, communitarians reject the specific qualities that liberal theorists often attribute to human nature. They reject liberal conceptions of the human condition primarily in terms of 'individualism, acquisitiveness, and, materialism ... '[10]

Franco's initial presentation of deontological liberalism and communitarianism in the rather sharp terms of an antinomy divides contemporary political theory into two mutually exclusive and irreconcilable camps (at least until the advent of Oakeshott's political philosophy). After setting out his demarcation, however, the sharpness of its character is qualified.

---

[8]   *Ibid.*, pp. 230–1.

[9]   *Ibid.*, p. 232.

[10] *Ibid.*, p. 235.

Hayek, for instance, 'grounds his liberal theory in a doctrine of procedural, non-purposive law rather than a doctrine of fundamental rights ... '[11] Some communitarians have displayed an awareness of liberal qualifications of the extreme deontological position. Thus, Franco observed that Rorty's initial rejection of Rawls's *A Theory of Justice*, on the grounds that it presents ahistorical criteria by which to justify and evaluate institutions disappears and 'Rorty now sees Rawls not as attempting to found liberal political institutions on a metaphysical theory of the self ... but rather as grounding them in our shared intuitions about justice and our historical self-understanding.'[12] And Franco described Rorty's position as historicist though 'not necessarily relativist', thus acknowledging that Rorty as taking a more moderate position than the relativist extreme of some communitarians.[13] In fact, few thinkers can be found who do not, in some degree, bridge Franco's antinomy. So, deontological liberalism and communitarianism describe the virtually uninhabited extremes of a continuum, rather than the front lines of two massed camps of opposing and irreconcilable theory.

The fundamental issue raised by Franco's continuum concerns the adequacy of the liberal-communitarian framework in providing an account of the distinctive qualities of Oakeshott's political philosophy. Oakeshott's work is distinct in providing an unusually strong bridge between liberalism

---

[11] *Ibid.,.* 231.

[12] *Ibid.,* pp. 232–4. Rorty critiques Rawl's *A Theory of Justice* in *Philosophy and the Mirror of Nature.* However, in 'The Priority of Democracy to Philosophy' in *The Virginia Statute for Religious Freedom: Its Evolution and Consequences for American History,* (ed. M. Peterson and R. Vaughan) (Cambridge, Cambridge University Press, 1988) Rorty argues that Rawls's 'Justice as Fairness: Political not Metaphysical', *Philosophy and Public Affairs,* 14 (1985) constitutes a more historicist position than *A Theory of Justice.* See Franco, *The Political Philosophy of Michael Oakeshott,* pp. 232–5.

[13] Franco, *The Political Philosophy of Michael Oakeshott,* p. 234.

and communitarianism but, on this understanding, it is the same type of undertaking as others preoccupied with this debate. The liberal-communitarian framework focuses upon Oakeshott's achievement in providing a theory of civil association that answers liberal concerns about the deontological significance of individual freedom and also maintains a communitarian insistence upon the historicity of the individual. However, civil association provides only a necessary condition for exploring one's individuality; it is, by definition, outside the capabilities of civil association to distinguish between authentic and inauthentic expressions of individuality or to identify the terms in which a self ought to set about establishing its individuality. In understanding Oakeshott's work in a liberal-communitarian framework the focus invariably falls upon his account of the appropriate terms of association; other themes in and aspects of his account of morality are treated as interesting asides or eccentric quirks.

2. Religion and Poetry:
Oakeshott as Existentialist and More

Attending to Oakeshott's accounts of religious and poetic experience brings to the fore elements in his work that have not gone unnoticed by commentators on his work. Some have observed what they refer to as Existentialist themes running through his work. Describing his predecessor's inaugural lecture at the London School of Economics and Political Science, Kenneth Minogue remarked that 'Across the channel something not altogether dissimilar was then enjoying a vogue under the name Existentialism … '[14] Noël O'Sullivan has also found strong thematic resonances between Oakeshott's account of the human condition and that offered by existent-

---

[14]   K.R. Minogue, 'Michael Oakeshott: The Boundless Sea of Politics', *Contemporary Political Philosophers*, (ed. A. de Crespigny and K.R. Minogue) (London, Methuen, 1976), pp. 121–2.

ialists, but notes that the former avoids the grandiloquent 'expressions of alienation, absurdity, angst and nausea associated with' the latter.[15] Grant and Flathman have both located the source of Oakeshott's affinity with existentialism in his idea of self-enactment.[16] And in his introduction to *Religion, Politics and the Moral Life* Timothy Fuller has found echoes of 'Arnold, but filtered through Kierkegaard, Nietzsche and Pater ... '[17] Gray even speculated that 'it may be that Oakeshott's thought points ... to a condition of postmodernity ... ', a pathology that echoes many of the themes developed in Existentialist thought.[18] While highly suggestive, these references occur as notes of interest (Minogue), the identification of possible avenues of exploration which are not followed up (O'Sullivan, Grant, Fuller and Gray) or in terms of a wider issue which does not specifically focus upon Oakeshott's work (Flathman).

Existentialism is a far reaching term which describes nothing so regular as a school of thought; it consists rather in a number of themes. The moods and styles of existentialist writers are many and varied. O'Sullivan has referred to expressions of alienation, absurdity, angst and nausea, however, Flathman has set out another side of existentialist thought in his account of 'strong voluntarism'. In strong voluntarism the emphasis on

> human doings and forgoings ... is always first and foremost on the wonder-ful quality or character of human conduct, on the ways in which our thinking and acting, in large part because they resist and finally defeat our own best efforts to

[15] N.K. O'Sullivan, 'In the Perspective of Western Thought', *The Achievement of Michael Oakeshott*, p. 102.

[16] See Grant, *Oakeshott*, p. 77 and Flathman, *Willful Liberalism*, p. 88.

[17] *Religion, Politics and the Moral Life*, p. 1.

[18] Gray, *Liberalism*, p. 213.

explain and understand them, ought to inspire wonderment in us.'[19]

Grant captures the existentialist core of Oakeshott's civil philosophy in the following way:

> 'We don't feel at home' wrote Rilke in the first *Duino Elegy* 'in this interpreted world.' But for Oakeshott … we should, first because (as Rilke eventually concluded) it is 'our world', in that we have made it, and secondly because there is no other.[20]

The self is the creator of its world and so itself. The existential self, unanchored by any hierarchy (angelic or otherwise), is a wonderful being. Oakeshott also acknowledged the limits of human powers of creation. Human being is a mortal condition; human creation is not eternal. We live in our world, but it is a world of limits whose character remains mysterious and an appropriate attitude to mystery is wonder.

Oakeshott's account of the self reflects many aspects that might be called existentialist. The idea of eternity or salvation in the present and the self-creative qualities and limitations identified by Hobbes, which Oakeshott himself referred to as pre-empting twentieth century existentialist thought, support these observations. In couching his most comprehensive characterisation of the self in terms of religious experience, however, there remains an echo of the British Idealist thinker whose influence so heavily weighed on Oakeshott's early work, particularly his writings on religion. In his Concluding Remarks to *Ethical Studies* F. H. Bradley wrote

> In the religious consciousness we find the belief, however vague and indistinct, in an object, a not-myself; an object, further, which is real. An ideal which is not real [which remains

---

[19]   Flathman, *Willful Liberalism*, pp. 9–10.

[20]   Grant, *Oakeshott*, p. 110.

an 'is to be'], which remains in our heads, cannot be the object of religion … [21]

The fact of Oakeshott's persistence in employing the idiom of religious experience to describe a self in its most comprehensive terms reflects his rejection of the solipsistic tendencies in some existentialist thought that has given rise to the language of absurdity, alienation and angst identified by O'Sullivan.

Oakeshott's thought is existentialist in giving serious attention to the predicament in which selves find themselves and the quality of responses these selves make to this predicament. However Oakeshott, like Hobbes before him, did not dwell upon the self as an isolated identity adrift in a meaningless universe or out of contact with an otherwise meaningful cosmos. He set out to understand both how a self becomes itself as well as how it communicates this self to other selves who find themselves in the same predicament, but who may respond in very different manners. In entering upon Oakeshott's considerations on these matters we come to his widely acclaimed account of the character of the appropriate terms of association. In exploring Oakeshott's account of civil and enterprise association and the various styles of politics that may encourage one or other of these modes, not only do we find an account of the appropriate character of relations between selves, but a statement of the adequacy of authority and desirability as principles of identity.

The importance of poetic experience in Oakeshott's work also resonates with the strong literary qualities of much of the writing in which existentialist themes have been developed in, for instance, the work of Kierkegaard, Dostoevski, Nietzsche, Sartre, Camus and Beckett. For Oakeshott, poetic experience is not just a subject for consideration in terms of the presuppositions it implies about the character of experience – the project of Oakeshott's best known statement on the character of poetic

---

[21] Bradley, *Ethical Studies*, p. 316.

experience in 'The Voice of Poetry'. His account of poetic experience as referring to the interior condition or sensibility of a self, is perhaps more identifiably existentialist than his account of religious experience precisely because in poetic experience there is even less of a sense of, in Bradley's phrase, a not-myself than in religion. However, as a frame of reference in which to explore the self-understandings that a society has of itself in terms of its myths and collective dream, Oakeshott's account of poetic experience goes beyond the existentialist focus on self to explore the self beyond even its social context — to consider its predicament as a situation that is common to all humanity.

A final noteworthy consequence of considering Oakeshott's account of conduct as a characterisation of the good life rather than primarily in terms of moral association is the location of the individual and the anti-individual at the centre of his undertaking. Rather than the individual and the anti-individual occurring as characters on the periphery of his work, characters that ground his treatment of the modes of association in an historical event, the modes of association now occur as one among a number of defining features that each of these characters imply about the character of conduct. The individual and the anti-individual are not solely concerned with the appropriate terms in which an association is constituted; they are not merely concerned with the virtue of justice understood as the maintenance of order within a state however conceived. On considering the individual and the anti-individual, justice is joined not only by honour but by the other cardinal virtues — wisdom, temperance and courage. And with these, their corresponding vices — pride, folly, excess and cowardice.

In according primary attention to Oakeshott's characterisation of the individual and the anti-individual, the manner in which his work is considered becomes less abstract. Like Oakeshott's consideration of Hobbes's *Leviathan* as a work of art in the proper sense, his own work can be seen as the product not only of an incisive mind but an expansive one. Oakeshott's work is itself a re-telling of the myth of original sin and a caution against the folly of pride – it is a contribution to the collective dream. His presentation revels in the contingencies of the modern European condition as responses to the more permanent predicament accompanying humanity as a creature that is imperfectible but can conceive (or at least deceive itself that it can conceive) of its perfection.

Bibliography

1. Oakeshott's Works

'Work and play', (Unpublished, n. d.)

A Discussion of Some Matters Preliminary to the Study of Political Philosophy, (Unpublished, 1925)

'Shylock the Jew: An Essay in Villainy', *Caian*, 30 (Michaelmas, 1921)

Experience and Its Modes, (Cambridge, Cambridge University Press, 1933). [Reprinted 1985]

'Thomas Hobbes', *Scrutiny*, 4 (1935-6)

'The Concept of a Philosophical Jurisprudence', *Politica*, 3 (1938)

Review of R.G. Collingwood, *The Principles of Art*, in *Cambridge Review*, 59 (1937-8)

Review of J. Lavrin, *Nietzsche*, in *Cambridge Journal*, 1 (1947-8)

Hobbes of Civil Association, (Oxford, Basil Blackwell, 1975

On Human Conduct, (Oxford, Clarendon Press, 1975)

'The Vocabulary of a Modern European State', *Political Studies*, 23 (1975)

'On Misunderstanding Human Conduct: A Reply to My Critics', *Political Theory*, 4 (1976)

On History and Other Essays, (Oxford, Basil Blackwell, 1983)

The Voice of Liberal Learning: Michael Oakeshott on Education, (Ed. T. Fuller) (New Haven, Yale University Press, 1989)

Rationalism in Politics and Other Essays, (New and expanded edition) (Ed. T. Fuller) (Indianapolis, Liberty Press, 1991)

Morality and Politics in Modern Europe: The Harvard Lectures, (1958) (Ed. S. R. Letwin) (New Haven, Yale University Press, 1993)

Religion, Politics and the Moral Life, (Ed. T. Fuller) (New Haven, Yale University Press, 1993)

The Politics of Faith and the Politics of Scepticism, (Ed. T. Fuller) (New Haven, Yale University Press, 1996)

2. Other Works

P. Anderson, 'The Intransigent Right at the Turn of the Century', *London Review of Books*, (24 September 1992)

Anselm, *Cur Deus Homo*, (Edinburgh, John Grant, 1909)

J.L. Auspitz, 'Individuality, Civility and Theory: the Philosophical Imagination of Michael Oakeshott', *Political Theory*, 4 (1976)

J. G. Blumler, 'Politics, Poetry and Practice', *Political Studies*, 12 (1964)

D. Boucher, 'Overlap and Autonomy: The Different Worlds of Collingwood and Oakeshott', *Storia, antropologia e scienze del linguaggio*, 4 (1989)

—, 'Politics in a Different Mode: An Appreciation of Michael Oakeshott, *History of Political Thought*, 12 (1991)

F. H. Bradley, *Appearance and Reality*, (London, Sonnenschein, 1893).

—, *The Principles of Logic*, Second edition and revised two volumes (London, Oxford University Press, 1922)

G.K. Chesterton, *St. Francis of Assisi*, (London, Hodder and Stroughton, 1923)

A. Cocks, 'Understanding the Real Oakeshott', *Quadrant*, (November, 1994).

R.G. Collingwood, *Speculum Mentis: or the Map of Knowledge*, (Oxford, Oxford University Press, 1924)

B. Crick, 'The World of Michael Oakeshott: Or the Lonely Nihilist', *Encounter*, 20 (June 1963)

C. Falck, 'Romanticism in Politics', *New Left Review*, 18 (January-February 1963)

R.E. Flathman, *The Practice of Political Authority: Authority and the Authoritative*, (Chicago, University of Chicago Press, 1980)

—, *Toward a Liberalism . . .*, (Ithaca, Cornell University Press, 1989)

—, *Willful Liberalism: Voluntarism and Individuality in Political Theory and Practice*, (Ithaca, Cornell University Press, 1992)

—, *Thomas Hobbes: Skepticism, individuality and chastened politics*, (Newbury Park, Sage Publications, 1993)

P. Franco, *The Political Philosophy of Michael Oakeshott*, (New Haven, Yale University Press, 1990)

S.A. Gerencser, 'Mister Oakeshott's Hobbes or Mister Hobbes's Oakeshott', (Unpublished paper presented at the American Political Science Association, August 1997; published in a revised form in S.A. Gerencser, *The Skeptic's Oakeshott* (New York: Palgrave Macmillan, 2000)).

R. Grant, *Oakeshott*, (London, Claridge Press, 1990)

—, 'Inside the Hedge: Oakeshott's Early Life and Work', Cambridge Review, 112 (1991)

—, 'Life Overflowing', *Times Literary Supplement*, (15 April 1994)

W.H. Greenleaf, *Oakeshott's Philosophical Politics*, (London, Longmans, 1966)

D. Hall and T. Modood, "Practical Politics and Philosophical Inquiry: A Note', *Philosophical Quarterly*, 29 (1979)

D. Hall and T. Modood, 'Oakeshott and the impossibility of philosophical politics', *Political Studies*, 30 (1982)

174   *Religious and Poetic Experience in Oakeshott*

G. W. F. Hegel, *The Phenomenology of Spirit*, (trans. A. V. Miller) (Oxford, Oxford University Press, 1977)

—, *The Philosophy of Right*, (trans. T. M. Knox) (London, Encyclopaedia Britannica, 1952)

E. Heller, *The Importance of Nietzsche: Ten: Essays*, (Chicago, University of Chicago Press, 1988)

T. Hobbes, *Leviathan*, (ed. M. Oakeshott) (Oxford, Basil Blackwell, 1946)

J. Huizinga, *Homo Ludens: A Study of the Play-element in Culture*, (London, Routledge, 1949)

W. James, *The Varieties of Religious Experience: A Study in Human Nature*, (London, Longmans, 1911)

H.H. Joachim, *The Nature of Truth* 2nd edition (London, Oxford University Press, 1939)

G. Johnson, Review of *The Voice of Poetry in the Conversation of Mankind*, in *Poetry Review*, 51 (1960)

S. Kiekegaard, *Fear and Trembling: A Dialectical Lyric*, (Trans. A. Hannay) (Harmondsworth, Penguin, 1985)

S.R. Letwin, 'Morality and law', *Ratio Juris*, 2 (March 1989)

J. Mack, 'The LSE: A Monument to Fabian Socialism?', *New Society*, 44 (15 June 1978)

K. Marx, *Early Writings*, (Harmondsworth, Penguin, 1975)

J. Milton, *Poetical Works*, (ed. D. Bush) (Oxford, Oxford University Press, 1966)

T. Modood, 'Oakeshott's conceptions of philosophy', *History of Political Thought*, 1 (1980)

C. Morris, *The Discovery of the Individual: 1050-1200*, (London, SPCK for the Church Historical Society, 1972)

R.L. Nettleship, *The Philosophical Remains of Richard Lewis Nettleship*, 2nd edition (ed. A.C. Bradley) (London, Macmillan 1901)

P.P. Nicholson, *The Political Philosophy of the British Idealists: Selected studies*, (Cambridge, Cambridge University Press, 1989)

F. Nietzsche, *The Portable Nietzsche*, (Ed. W. Kaufmann) (Harmondsworth, Viking Press, 1968)

J. Norman (Ed.) *The Achievement of Michael Oakeshott*, (London, Duckworth, 1993)

R. Orr, 'A Double Agent in the Dream of Michael Oakeshott', *Political Science Reviewer*, 21 (1994)

N.K. O'Sullivan, *The Problem of Political Obligation in the Writings of T.H. Green, B. Bosanquet and M. Oakeshott*, (New York, Garland Press, 1987)

H.F. Pitkin, 'Inhuman Conduct and Unpolitical Theory: Michael Oakeshott's *On Human Conduct*', *Political Theory*, 4 1976)

D.D. Raphael, 'Professor Oakeshott's *Rationalism in Politics*', *Political Studies*, 12 (1964)

P. Riley, 'Michael Oakeshott, Political Philosopher', *Cambridge Review*, 112 (October 1991)

A. Schopenhauer, *Essays from the Parerga and Paralimpomena*, (Trans. T. Bailey Saunders) (London, Allen and Unwin, 1951)

R. Scruton (Ed.), *Conservative Thinkers: Essays from The Salisbury Review*, (London, Claridge Press, 1988)

P.B. Shelley, *The Complete Poetical Works of P. B. Shelley*, (ed. T. Hutchinson) (London, Oxford University Press, 1948)

Q. Skinner, 'The ideological context of Hobbes's political thought', *The Historical Journal*, 9 (1969)

—, 'Warrender and Skinner: A Reply', *Political Studies*, 36 (1979).

C. Taylor, *Hegel*, (Cambridge, Cambridge University Press, 1975)

Theresa of Ávila, *Complete Works of St. Theresa*, 3 volumes (ed. E. A. Peers) (London, Sheed and Ward, 1975)

A. Vincent and R. Plant, *Philosophy, Politics and Citizenship: The life and thought of the British Idealists*, (Oxford, Basil Blackwell, 1984)

H. Warrender, *The Political Philosophy of Thomas Hobbes: His Theory of Obligation*, (Oxford, Clarendon Press, 1957)

—, 'Political Theory and Historiography : A Reply to Professor Skinner', *The Historical Journal*, 22 (1979)

L. Wittgenstein, *Tractatus Logico-Philosophicus*, (trans. C.K. Ogden) (London, 1922).

R. Wollheim, *F.H. Bradley*, (Harmondsworth, Peregrine, 1969).

Index